Anna

from Julian Budden

Xmas 1956

TO SOOTHE A SAVAGE BREAST

By the same Author:

MUSIC IN THE FIVE TOWNS
ORDEAL BY MUSIC
THE ORCHESTRA IN ENGLAND
WHILE THE ORCHESTRA ASSEMBLES

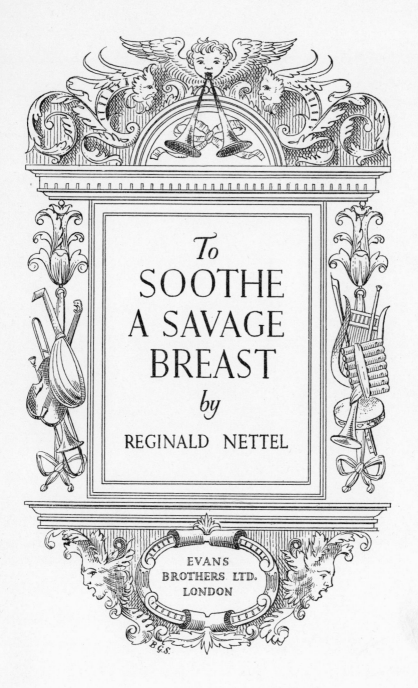

To
SOOTHE
A SAVAGE
BREAST

by

REGINALD NETTEL

EVANS
BROTHERS LTD.
LONDON

First published 1950

PRINTED IN GREAT BRITAIN BY
CHISWICK PRESS, NEW SOUTHGATE, N.11

TO
E. STUART
CARTWRIGHT

CONTENTS

PREFACE

THIS BOOK is intended for those who have a good eye for English prose and an ear for music. It follows an historical pattern, but it is not a history of music; all the book does is to put together a series of opinions on music and life, each able to be read for its own appeal, but made more interesting by comparison with the thoughts of other writers. Here are letters, essays, sermons, and passages from treatises, diaries and novels: some well known, others available if sought, and a few not previously available to the general reader. I have not tried to strike a just balance of different opinions, and still less to choose passages that can be made to serve any form of propaganda; my own thoughts on the theme are expressed in the chapters at the head of the three sections of the book—I repeat—my own thoughts, for I do not wish for any reader to accept them as a substitute for his own.

I have found this collection of opinions useful in my relations with adult educational groups, where it has often stimulated an interest in English music through the questions that spring to mind when different aspects of the same theme are discussed, and others might like to use it in this way, or as an aid to literary appreciation among music students. I have also found it a good bedtime book—at least in those parts that I have not written myself—and if it appeals to any other reader in this way I shall be happy. Lest it should be thought that a good collection of bedtime prose is by its nature unsuitable for adult education, I hasten to point out that the prose passages I have chosen are to be savoured, not studied in the textbook sense, and that in my view the savouring of literature and music is the object of these forms of culture.

I acknowledge my indebtedness to all the writers whose works are quoted herein, and to the following owners of copyright:

Messrs. Macmillan and the Trustees of the Thomas Hardy Estate, for permission to quote the passage from *Under the Greenwood Tree*; Messrs. John Lane, The Bodley Head, for Charles Willeby's essay on *The Composer of "Carmen"*; and Messrs. Jonathan Cape Ltd., for the extract from Samuel Butler's *Erewhon*.

1949.   R. N.

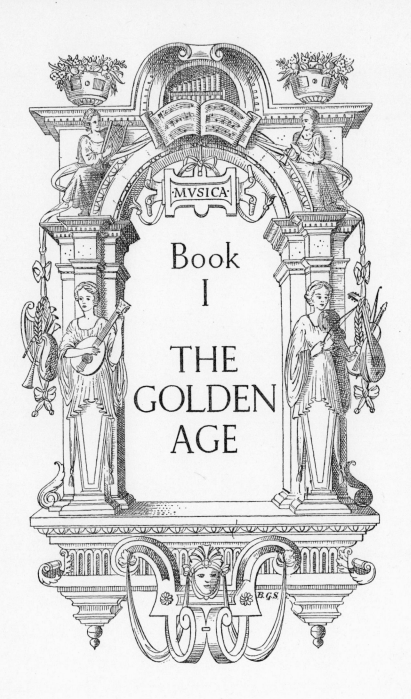

MVSICA

Book
I

THE
GOLDEN
AGE

THE GOLDEN AGE

AMONG THE passages in English prose that I most treasure is one in Izaak Walton's *Life of Mr. George Herbert*, telling how Mr. Herbert came one day into a company of his musical friends soiled and discomposed after helping a poor man to load his horse; and being told by one of the company that he had disparaged himself with so dirty an employment, the honest parson-poet replied that "the thought of what he had done would prove music to him at midnight, and that the omission of it would have upbraided him and made discord in his conscience."

I know of no more simple way of showing understanding of the nature of concord and discord than this. Music to George Herbert was more than a sweet arrangement of sounds—it was a mental state. And because he thought of it in this way he was able to use music as a symbol of his way of life, accepting the theory that conflicts could be reconciled, and in the reconciliation rendered beautiful, as discords in music may resolve in pleasing harmonies.

> Sweetest of sweets, I thank you! when displeasure
> Did through my body wound my mind,
> You took me hence, and in your house of pleasure
> A dainty lodging me assigned.

But there was something more. George Herbert had a way of regarding music as a living thing, distinct from himself. I do not mean by this that he and his companions would be so foolish as to deny that they themselves set the viols sounding, or that the music would be there if they could not hear it, but that their music had a pure impersonal beauty such as was created by no other human activity:

Now I in you without a body move,
   Rising and falling with your wings;
We both together sweetly live and love,
   Yet say sometimes, "God help poor kings!"

George Herbert had church music in mind when he wrote this poem, but the thought was nevertheless apt for the style of playing he and his friends cultivated in their meetings twice a week. The music they played on their viols would be composed of an effective melodic part for each player, the joy being in the interweaving of these parts without any effort of personal aggrandisement, so that the lines of melody made a "consort". He would have agreed with Shakespeare:

Mark how one string, sweet husband to another,
Strikes each in each by mutual ordering;
Resembling sire and child and happy mother,
Who, all in one, one pleasing note do sing:
   Whose speechless song, being many, seeming one,
   Sings this to thee: "Thou single wilt prove none."

The stringed instruments they used were provided with frets, as is a guitar; the players did not cultivate vibrato or other means of affecting throbbing emotionalism. If they used wind instruments the type used would be the recorder, a soft fipple-flute—again with an even tone. If they sang, the parts would interweave with the same impersonal beauty—vibrato or striving for personal supremacy would have been regarded as marring the consort. Though one of them would direct the consort, he would be one of the fellowship in the resulting music, and no more. Therein lay the charm that George Herbert saw in music, and its association in his mind with the Christian virtues of humility and consideration for one's friends, knit together by the all-embracing love of God, can be understood. This was no abstract affectation, but a philosophy that fitted the conception of society in which George Herbert and his friends believed.

No account of this society would be adequate if it failed to take into consideration the force of conscience that was growing in men at that time. When George Herbert resolved to enter holy orders a friend at Court told him that such a course was ill-advised, as such a calling was too mean for one of his birth and intellectual ability. Such a point of view is consistent with Shakespeare's characterisation of some of the clergy, and their status had altered little by Herbert's time. Yet Herbert answered in much the same strain as he answered the man who blamed him for the mean employment of helping the poor carrier. "It hath been formerly adjudged that the domestic servants of the King of Heaven should be of the noblest families on earth; and though the iniquity of the late times have made clergymen meanly valued, and the sacred name of priest contemptible, yet I will labour to make it honourable by consecrating all my learning, and all my poor abilities, to advance the glory of that God that gave them."[1] So long as men refused to admit that certain occupations should be limited strictly to certain social classes a flexibility resulted that has done good service to the British way of life. Of George Herbert's family his eldest brother was an ambassador to the French Court, his second and third brothers fought and died as soldiers in the Low Countries, the fourth was a Fellow of New College, Oxford; his brother Henry was Master of the Revels at the court of James I (which Walton calls being "a menial servant") and his youngest brother was a sea captain. The family of Herbert was one of the most honourable among the English gentry, yet they had this variety of occupations.

So it was also within the house. Domestic arts and crafts like the making of bread, cakes, and ale by the women, or elaborate needlework, were the general rule. There might be in a large household several non-menial servants—ladies who were related to the family and employed in household affairs, and men who were occupied with secretarial duties, or helping to manage the estate in other ways. They loved to use their imaginations in all kinds of ways, and indeed they had to, for the life they lived cut

---

[1] Izaak Walton: *Life of Mr. George Herbert.*

them off from a good many sources of fact which we today take for granted. News travelled by letter or by hearsay, reaching them always through subjective channels. There were no newspapers in the Elizabethan home, though the printing press had been established in England for over a century. People read Holinshed, poetry, fanciful romances in the pastoral tradition, and especially after 1611 the Bible: all couched in the rich language that belongs to an age with a good ear. At fairs the pedlars sang and sold their ballads, which told of current affairs and long-cherished legends with equal felicity. Ben Jonson could dress up a comedy with a ballad that went to the tune of *Pagging-ton's Pound*, and make it an essential part of the story. Such was the age—an age of imagination, when wonder surrounded every new fact that came over from the Indies, from Italy, Spain, or from the Court. Queen Elizabeth made prolonged journeys among her people, graced their houses and enjoyed their hospitality, and everywhere she went there was music and dancing. Merry England? Yes; for though there was as much evil in the world as at any other time, people had scope for initiative.

This was the golden age of music in England, though to be true it was not quite so golden as it has been gilded. There is a much-quoted passage from the beginning of Thomas Morley's *Plaine and Easie Introduction to Practicall Musicke*, that has been accepted very widely at its face value in recent years. The book is written in dialogue form, and one of the characters, named Philomathes, says:[1]

"Among the rest of the guests, by chaunce, master *Aphron* came hither also, who falling to discourse on Musicke, was in an argument so quickly taken up and hotly pursued by *Eudoxus* and *Calergus*, two kinsmen of *Sophobulus*, as in his own art he was overthrown. But he still sticking in his opinion, the two gentlemen requested me to examine his reasons, and confute them. But I refusing and pretending ignorance, the whole

[1] The origin of the idea quoted is in the *Libro del Cortegiano* by Castiglione, published in 1528. It is an idealised picture of the social life of the times.

company condemned me of discurtesie, being fully perswaded, that I had beene as skilfull in that art, as they took me to be learned in others. But supper being ended, and Musicke bookes (according to the custome) being brought to the tables, the mistresse of the house presented me with a part, earnestly requesting me to sing. But when, after many excuses, I protested unfainedly that I could not: every one began to wonder. Yea, some whispered to others, demaunding how I was brought up: so that upon shame of mine ignorance, I go now to seeke out mine old friend master *Gnorimus*, to make my selfe his scholler."

This is all right as far as it goes, provided we do not know the great difficulty of some of the music of the period; but ought the quotation to stop there, when the music-master appears, and the dialogue goes on:

Philomathes: "My errand is to you, to be your scholler."
Master: "You tell me a wonder: for I have heard you speake against that Art, as to tearme it a corrupter of good manners, and an allurement to vices: for which many of your companions tearmed you a *Stoick*."

There were, after all, people who liked music, and others who did not. The issue becomes confused during the seventeenth century as Puritan thought takes the offensive—a confusion aggravated by historians who have disliked Puritan thought, and little served by some who have endeavoured to condone everything the Puritans did. Opinion was a matter for the individual conscience in religion, and in music for the individual taste. Thomas Morley was a professional musician, concerned with the defence of his art against any opponent—especially, it would seem from his introductory letter *To the Curteous Reader*, opponents in his own profession—and anxious to spread the knowledge of his art. He begins his book with an appeal to the reader's imagination, in the true Elizabethan manner. William Byrd did

17

the same in his *Reasons briefely set downe by th'auctor, to perswade every one to learne to sing,* printed in his book of *Psalmes, Sonets & Songs of Sadnes and Pietie* in 1588. Byrd produces every kind of reason for singing: physical, educational, cultural and devout; but he does not pretend that singing at sight was a general accomplishment among the gentry; indeed he says that good voices are rare, and many that have them do not know how to use them. Opinions among professional musicians were pretty much the same; all were anxious to spread understanding and to improve standards of performance, but their lines of propaganda differed. Byrd produced reasons for believing that many benefits would come as a result of learning to sing; Morley tried to shame his less gifted readers into the necessary effort. Henry Peacham read both, and a good deal more besides, and in 1622 gave his own opinion in *The Compleat Gentleman.* His view is that of the amateur: know enough of music to entertain yourself in private, or in company with similarly-disposed friends, but do not seek to display your powers above your fellows; leave virtuosity for the professionals. Queen Elizabeth thought the same.

Yet because the Elizabethans and their successors so loved music, they were great patrons of professional musicians. Many of the best composers of the age lived with the gentry in their country houses, sharing in the non-menial duties of the establishment, and making their own distinctive contribution to the household's atmosphere. In some cases quite a large musical establishment was kept, an example being Hengrave Hall, the seat of Sir Thomas Kytson, where John Wilbye lived and made music for thirty years. (He also managed a sheep farm.) Outstanding men like John Bull, brilliant player on the virginals, and John Dowland the lutenist could not have attained the musical standards they did, had they not been given a large measure of encouragement to work in their own way, even though the resulting compositions were such as amateurs could not always perform. The madrigals of John Wilbye are often difficult to sing, the harmonic effects original and very beautiful, but the idea of amateurs singing them at sight is hardly tenable. Once we realise, however, that there would be trained singers available at Hengrave Hall to do justice to these madrigals, the problem is eased. When Byrd and Morley advocated the singing of madrigals by amateurs more widely, they were doing what outstanding musicians have often been led to do in order to make their music more widely known; and like so many composers even today, they came up against the necessity for improved standards of amateur performance if their works were to be done at all in this way. Peacham is a retailer of opinions: he would not have men spend too much time and effort on music, and desired no more than that his readers should sing their part sure and at first sight in the privacy of their own homes, either not knowing the amount of skill needed to sing sure and at first sight, or accepting a standard of performance that would not satisfy his "*Phoenix*, M. William Byrd", or any other of the English musicians he so rightly praises.

Yet Peacham's tittle-tattle round and about music and manners is a better guide to the spirit of the age than the prose writings of musicians. There in Peacham is the curiosity and wonder of the age: not a childlike wonder, that is held in suspense at the marvel without passing on to an interpretation, but a mature wonder that relates marvel to marvel, finding a harmony in delights of different natures. His little peeps at the mystery of resonance have all the character of discovery rather than of methodical research; his running-over the opinions of classical thinkers, without comment in most cases, has an air of revelling in these opinions for their own sake, and because they are the sort of thing a complete gentleman should know. The comparison of musical devices with literary devices entertains rather than instructs, and his reasons for loving the art are those which his friends would approve. Only when he gets on religious ground does Peacham really start to think; and the reason is not far to seek; the gentry were not in agreement here, and so he has to express himself carefully, and explain his views. In doing so he bows to the opinion of the unmusical, as a complete gentleman should, before condemning them. These things are of the nature of a conservative English gentleman, and Puritan tension that was to test them was already taking the strain.

So many were the joys of the mind in that last flowering of Renaissance thought, yet how familiar! The same blooms come again and again; the thoughts of Aristotle, Pindar and Pythagoras; tales of Cupid, Mercury and Philologia. One writer after another wraps them round with descriptions of soft soothing music, only too often without much knowledge of the art itself. Milton is an exception; he uses musical terms with understanding and love, though his advocacy of music for non-musical benefits makes us look hard at his motives. Rarely do these authors try to describe the music truly; they fan out into the trackless field of associated emotions, and find that thought can be related through their association even though each different art has to follow its own laws. Burton's *Anatomy of Melancholy* is a marvellous piece of erudition, standing as it does on the turn of thought towards modern science, but musicians will read it today for the humour of it. Humour in the modern sense of that word, not Burton's. "If once we be in love, young or old, though our teeth shake in our head like virginal jacks, or stand parallel asunder like the arches of a bridge, there is no remedy, we must dance trenchmore for a need, over tables, chairs, and stools, etc. And Princum Prancum is a fine dance."

What does he mean? Virginal jacks we understand. They were the little wooden mechanism holding the quills by which the strings were plucked, though Shakespeare seems to think they are the keys of the instrument:

> How oft, when thou, my music, music play'st,
> Upon that blessed wood whose motion sounds
> With thy sweet fingers, when thou gently sway'st
> The wiry concord that mine ear confounds,
> Do I envy those jacks that nimble leap
> To kiss the tender inward of thy hand,

and *Trenchmore* we know as a country-dance tune; but what is all this about dancing over tables and stools, even though one is getting on in years? Is this the behaviour of a gentleman? Apparently for a time it was, during the period of Buckingham's ascendency, and before things got too hot for Charles the First. Yet tradition held together certain customs in social activities whatever the times. The gentlemen of the various Inns of Court had held what were called solemn revels from All-Hallows to Ascentiontide by decree since the time of Edward IV, at which dancing had always been a feature. It was to these young lawyers that John Playford addressed his preface to *The Dancing Master* in 1651. "The Art of Dancing is a commendable and rare Quality fit for young gentlemen . . . that has been formerly honoured at the Courts of Princes, when performed by the Gentlemen at the Innes of Court, whose sweet and ayry Activity has crowned their Grand Solemnities with Admiration to all Spectators." The Commonwealth had arrived, but the Country Dances that Playford describes in his book were not forbidden: this was an age of alleged inviolability of the individual conscience; alleged but not actual, however, for dances might be criticised on religious grounds. Maypole and Morris had pagan associations that were condemned by the Puritans.

It had not always been so.[1] In the time of Henry VII (according to the Fairfax MS.) a Morris might "come in incontinent" between two of the courtly dances of a Masque. Originally the Masque had been a social entertainment that later became a sort of social ritual. The first Masques consisted of a procession of visiting friends, disguised, who arrived dressed in fine costumes and danced before the company. There was no singing or spoken dialogue. This formed the "main" of the Masque. Then the party withdrew in another dance of a processional character. In the reign of Henry VIII the custom was established for the visiting maskers, still disguised, to invite the lady spectators to dance, strictly in order of social precedence, after which the maskers revealed their identity, before withdrawing in their

[1] See Margaret Dean-Smith and E. J. Nicol: *The Dancing Master*, 1651-1728. Journal of the English Folk Dance and Song Society, Vol. IV, Nos. 4, 5 and 6.

final dance or "movement". James I liked a Masque but could not dance: he therefore watched while his Queen danced. The effect of the king being outside the company of dancers while remaining by right the centre of the social picture, was to emphasise the importance of the non-dancing spectator. This was the great age of the English Masque as a spectacle. Between the courtly dances custom demanded contrasted dances by professionals, called the Antimasque. The characters of the Antimasque were grotesque—Francis Bacon gives his views in his essay *Of Masques and Triumphs*—but being experts they could be given more elaborate entertaining to do. Music, songs and dialogue were added to the dumb show of the earliest Masques, and the great spectacles of the Jacobean age evolved under the influence of an outstanding artistic partnership consisting of Inigo Jones, who devised the spectacle, Ben Jonson, who wrote the dialogue, and Thomas Campian, who wrote the music. Praise of the king, as the centre of the social scheme, was an essential of these performances; gods and allegorical characters alike vied in flattery of the monarch. When at the Restoration Dryden turned his attention to the opera, his work was still bound up with the thought of the monarch as the principal benefactor, who must be complimented by inference constantly by the characters on the stage. In *Albion and Albanius* the name-parts represent Charles II and his brother James.

The Preface to this opera is a document important in the history of opera, for in it Dryden tries to outline the scope of this new art. He rightly attributes it to the Italian gentry, mentioning Guarini's *Pastor Fido* as a true precursor, which it is, though he apparently failed to get information about the earliest operas of Caccini, Peri and Monteverdi. Dryden is still apt to rely on his imagination when truth demands a more scientific approach. He pleads the cause of his composer Grabu, a bad French composer whose inferior music and superior standing in court favour were rightly resented by British composers; he regards with disfavour the English language, though Henry Purcell was later, in *King Arthur*, to show him how our tongue could be set to

music distinctively; but above all he seems to have lost touch with
the common-sense English humour in artificial art-conventions.
Shakespeare could play with the pastoral tradition, mixing court
characters with true rustics and artificial shepherds in such a play
as *As You Like It,* and the audience was amused even while
enjoying the convention: but in the preface to *Albion and
Albanius* Dryden has lost the touch, for he seems to believe the
absurdity that sheep-rearing is an idle employment, leaving
shepherds and shepherdesses with time on their hands for everlasting love-making, and therefore fit to appear in an opera along
with gods and heroes. Only by distorting social facts out of
recognition can Dryden satisfy the taste of a court that has changed
since the days of Elizabeth, and has come under the domination—
not merely the influence—of France. The English genius is
under attack.

Yet it need not have been so. William Lawes had felt the tug
of a new spirit in art. The delights of folksong blended with the
indoor music of the gentry were not for him. Variations on
The Carman's Whistle and *Sellinger's Round* for the virginals
suited Byrd's temperament but not that of William Lawes.
George Herbert's fondness for the viols—for the pure impersonal
beauty of music in which the player lost himself—could not
forever satisfy a composer who strove to bend fine music to
the will of a brilliant court accustomed to elaborate masques and
admiration of individual merit in performers. Lawes composed
in the English tradition of imaginative fancies, and was quite
as experimental as the madrigalists, but his genius led him towards
the violin and away from the viols. This was a natural development such as happened abroad, but the English amateurs looked
askance at it for a long time. Fuller writes with reverence of
William Lawes (though he does not apparently know that his
master Coperario was English) but Anthony Wood tells us what
the English amateur musician thought of the new fashion.

Did Anthony know of the use Thomas Campian made of
violins in the most courtly of his masques? Perhaps. Nevertheless the fiddler was to Anthony Wood a common musician not

to be admitted to gentlemen's company, until Sir Anthony Cope, of Hanwell near Banbury, entertained Baltzar, the great violin virtuoso; then the company of Oxford players on the older instruments had perforce to bow to his superior accomplishment. Yet there comes from Anthony a note of regret, very English in its appeal. "Mr. Davis Mell was accounted hitherto the best for the violin in England, as I have before told you; but after Baltzar came into England and shewed his most wonderful parts on that instrument, Mell was not so admired; yet he played sweeter, and was a well bred gentleman and not given to excessive drinking as Baltzar was."

What is a well-bred gentleman? Davie Mell was by trade a clockmaker. Anthony Wood took behaviour into consideration when he spoke of a gentleman. Samuel Pepys, too, is guided by behaviour. Pelham Humfrey may have been a young popin-jay, but was he a bad musician, as Pepys implies? There is a danger in accepting amateur opinion on music and musicians, but the gain in understanding of music's place in the social scheme offsets the danger. It also offsets the danger of biased professional opinions. We are not impressed when the youthful Pelham Humfrey says that Grebus (Grabus or Grabu) understands nothing, and that he will give him a lift out of his place, but we take notice when Pepys himself hears Grabu's music, praises the precision of his orchestra, but dislikes his vocal composition, and we can realise how Dryden had to take sides with Grabu to defend *Albion and Albanius*. No; the opinions of artists are in their way as unreliable as those of amateurs, but the two played off against each other allow of the reader drawing his own conclusion with a better understanding of the nature of truth than he will get from either taken alone.

Yet the function of an art is not to balance judgments and weigh criticisms, but to create beauty. How can this beauty be true if it ignores the actualities of life? The fact is that those who love beauty earnestly try to make it part of their lives. George Herbert saw harmony in music that he had to bring into tune with his daily behaviour; Henry Peacham tried to produce a harmony between the social values of music and his theories of its performance; Anthony Wood and Samuel Pepys are more accurate in observation than earlier writers, and less given to special pleading, but still in them we can see the harmony of thought being cultivated as an end beautiful in itself. It may even be urged that the greatest satisfaction comes when personal aspirations are related in the mind with what one believes to be good art. When Thomas Lodge wrote *Rosalynde. Euphues Golden Legacie*, he produced a flowery pastoral story that we cannot greatly admire ourselves, but which serves to remind us of the genius of Shakespeare, who could humanise such a tale into the play of *As You Like It*. Lodge's characters sing their painful ditties, such as Shakespeare's Jaques must have had in mind when he told Amiens he did not desire him to please, he did desire him to sing. But the audience at a playhouse was more varied than the limited public for which Lodge wrote his pastoral: a greater range of humour was expected, and Shakespeare had the broader view that still vitalises his work. Lodge wrapped up his classical learning in flowery prose, and his readers were happy in a Golden Age that they never knew, but relegated to the past. They were not alone in their vision of a Golden Age: every man postulates some kind of ideal existence in his more imaginative moments, but need it be imagined as past and lost? John Bunyan did not long for a return to the Garden of Eden, but imagined a journey that would take him to a Golden Age of the future, the heavenly Jerusalem, inhabited by the innumerable company of angels, and (the addition is characteristic) the spirits of just men made perfect. In this imaginative heaven he achieves the harmony of conscience and understanding for which he sought. His learning is satisfied by constant references to biblical texts, his holy men find happiness in a state designed exclusively for holy men, in which praise and thanksgiving are the principal needs of man. So they sing, surrounded by the heavenly trumpeters, and intoxicated with the sound of ringing bells, which in heaven cannot be sinful. Much has been made of Bunyan's musical angels, proving as they do that a good Puritan need not disdain music, but Bunyan's musical angels are seen in a dream; they are formed of a projected wish; they are free from the vices of vanity and spite that can be associated with music on earth; so Bunyan creates his harmony of the mind to which he would aspire, and sends it out among mankind in prose that gives this harmony to the world. Is he doing the musician's job in another medium? The answer is that surely this is not solely a musician's job, for harmony has a wider significance than its technical sense would allow; all civilised thought admits this, and the age in which Bunyan lived saw another more informed than he, whose mind ranged over a wider sweep of chords, but still maintained the mystic harmony. In one verse Milton could sweep from Pythagoras to the English consort:

> Ring out, ye crystal spheres!
> Once bless our human ears,
> If ye have power to touch our senses so;
> And let your silver chime
> Move in melodious time;
> And let the bass of heaven's deep organ blow;
> And with your ninefold harmony
> Make up full consort to the angelic symphony.

and though Newton might supplant Pythagoras, the thought of the mystic harmony must go on; did not Nicholas Brady provide the words of an *Ode for St. Cecilia's Day* for Henry Purcell, and in the doing of it say this?

> Soul of the world, inspired by thee
> The jarring seeds of matter did agree.
> Thou didst the scattered atoms bind,
> Which, by the laws of true proportion joined,
> Made up of various parts one perfect harmony.

William Byrd

REASONS BRIEFELY SET DOWNE BY TH'AUCTOR, TO PERSWADE EVERY ONE TO LEARNE TO SING.

FIRST, IT is a knowledge easily taught, and quickly learned, where there is a good Master, and an apt Scoller.

2 The exercise of singing is delightfull to Nature, & good to preserve the health of Man.

3 It doth strengthen all the parts of the brest, & doth open the pipes.

4 It is a singuler good remedie for a stutting & stamering in the speech.

5 It is the best meanes to procure a perfect pronunciation, & to make a good Orator.

6 It is the onely way to know where Nature hath bestowed the benefit of a good voyce: which guift is so rare, as there is not one among a thousand, that hath it: and in many, that excellent guift is lost, because they want Art to expresse Nature.

7 There is not any Musicke of Instruments whatsoever, comparable to that which is made of the voyces of Men, where the voices are good, and the same well sorted and ordered.

8 The better the voyce is, the meeter it is to honour and serve God there-with: and the voyce of man is chiefely to be imployed to that ende.

Omnis spiritus laudet Dominum.

Since singing is so good a thing,
I wish all men would learne to sing.

*Psalmes, Sonets & Songs of Sadnes
and Pietie.* 1588

Thomas Morley

TO THE CURTEOUS READER

I DO not doubt, but many (who have knowen my disposition in times past) will wonder that (amongst so manie excellent Musicians as be in our Country at this time, and farre better furnished with learning then my selfe) I have taken upon me to set out that in our vulgar tongue, which of all other things hath been in writing least knowen to our Countrimen, and most in practise. Yet if they would consider the reasons moving mee thereunto: they would not onely leave to mervaile, but also thinke me worthy, if not of praise, yet of pardon for my paines. First, the earnest intreatie of my friends daily requesting, importuning, and as it were adjuring me by the love of my Country, which next to the glory of God, ought to be most dear to every man. Which reason, so often tolde and repeated to mee by them, chiefly caused me yeald to their honest request, in taking in hand this worke which now I publish to the viewe of the world: Not so much seeking thereby any name of glory, (though no honest mind do contemne that also, and I might more largely by other meanes and less labour have obtained it) as in some sort to further the studies of them, who (being indewed with good naturall wits, and well inclined to learne that divine Art of Musicke) are destitute of sufficient masters. Lastly, the solitarie life which I lead (being compelled to keepe at home) caused me to be glad to finde any thing wherein to keepe my selfe exercised for the benefit of my Country. But as concerning the booke it selfe, if I had, before I began it, imagined halfe the paines and labour which it cost me, I would sooner have beene perswaded

28

to any thing, then to have taken in hand such a tedious peece
of worke, like to a great Sea, which the further I entred into the
more I sawe before me unpast: So that at length despairing ever
to make an end (seeing that grow so bigge in my hands, which I
thought to have shut up in two or three sheetes of paper) I laid
it aside, in full determination to have proceeded no further, but
to have left it off as shamefully as it was foolishly begun. But
then being admonished by some of my friends, that it were pittie
to lose the fruits of imployment of so many good houres, and
how justly I should be condemned of ignorant presumption in
taking that in hand which I could not performe, if I did not go
forward: I resolved to endure whatsoever paine, labour, losse
of time and expence (and what not?) rather than to leave that
unbrought to an end, in the which I was so farre ingulfed.
Taking therefore those precepts which being a child I learned,
and laying them together in order, I began to compare them
with some other of the same kind, set downe by some late writers:
But then was I in a worse case than before, For I found such
diversitie betwixt them, that I knew not which part said truest,
or whom I might best beleeve. Then was I forced to runne to
the workes of many, both strangers and Englishmen (whose
labours together with their names had beene buried with me in
perpetual oblivion, if it had not beene for this occasion) for a
solution and clearing of my doubt. But to my great grief, then
did I see the most part of mine own precepts, false and easie
to be confuted by the works of Taverner, Fairfax, Cooper, and
infinite more, whose names it would be too tedious to set downe
in this place. But what labour it was to tumble, tosse, and search
so many bookes, and with what toil and wearinesse I was
enforced to compare the parts for trying out the valure of
some notes (spending whole daies, yea and many times weekes
for the demonstration of one example, which one would have
thought might in a moment be set downe) I leave to thy discretion to consider: and none can fully understand, but he who
hath had or shall have occasion to do the like. As for the methode
of the booke, although it be not such as may in every point

satisfie the curiositie of *Dichotomists;* yet is it such as I thought most convenient for the capacitie of the learner. And I have had an especiall care, that nothing should be set out of its owne place, but that it which should serve to the understanding of that which followeth should be set first. And as for the definition, division, parts, and all kinds of Musicke, I have omitted them as things onely serving to content the learned, and not for the instruction of the ignorant. Thus hast thou the reasons which moved me to take in hand and go forward with the booke. The paines of making whereof, though they have beene peculiar to me, yet will the profit redound to a great number. And this much I may boldly affirme, that any of but meane capacity, so that they can but truly sing their tunings, which we commonly call the six notes, or ut, re, *mi*, fa, sol, la, may without any other helpe saving this booke, perfectly learne to sing, make descant, and set parts well and formally together. But seeing in these latter daies and doting age of the world, there is nothing more subject to calumnie and backbiting than that which is most true and right; and that as there be many who will enter into the reading of my booke for their instruction; so I doubt not but diverse also will read it, not so much for any pleasure or profit they look for in it, as to find some thing whereat to repine, or take occasion for backbiting. Such men I warne, that if in friendship they will (either publickely or privately) make mee acquainted with any thing in the booke, which either they like not or understand not, I will not onely give them a reason (and if I cannot, to turne to their opinion) but also thinke my selfe highly beholding to them. But if any man, either upon malice, or for ostentation of his owne knowledge, or for ignorance (as who is more bold than blind Bayard?) do either in hugger-mugger or openly calumniate that which either he understandeth not, or then maliciously wresteth to his own sense, hee (as *Augustus* said by one, who had spoken evil of him) shall find that I have a tongue also: and that *me remorsurum petit*, He snarleth at one who will bite again; because I have said nothing without reason, or at least confirmed by the authorities of the best, both schollers and practitioners.

There have also beene some, who (knowing their owne insufficiencie, and not daring to disallow, nor, being able to improve any thing in the booke) have neverthelesse gone about to discredite both me and it another way; affirming that I have by setting out thereof maliciously gone about to take the livings from a number of honest poore men, who live (and that honestly) upon teaching not halfe of that which in this booke may be found. But to answer those malicious caterpillers (who live upon the paines of other men) this booke will be so farre from the hinderance of any, that by the contrarie, it will cause those whom they alledge to be thereby damnified, to be more able to give reason for that which they do: whereas, before, they either did it at haphazard, or for (all reasons alledged) that they were so taught. So that if any at all owe me any thanks for the great paines which I have taken, they be in my judgement, those who taught that which they knew not, and may here if they will learne. But if the effect do not answere to any good meaning: and if many do not reape that benefit which I hoped; yet there will be no reason why I should be blamed, who have done what I could, and given an occasion to others of better judgement and deeper skill then my selfe to do the like. And as for those ignorant Asses, who take upon them to lead others, none being more blind than themselves, and yet without any reason (before they have seen their works) will condemn other men, I overpasse them, as unworthie to be nominated, or that any man should vouchsafe to answer them: for they be indeede such as doing wickedly hate the light, for feare they should be espied. And so, gentle Reader, hoping by thy favourable curtesie, to avoid both the malice of the envious and the temeritie of the ignorant, wishing thee the whole profit of this booke, and all perfection in thy studies, I rest,

Thine, in all curtesie,
Tho. Morley.

A Plaine and Easie Introduction to
Practicall Musicke.

William Shakespeare

MELANCHOLY IDYLL

Amiens. Under the greenwood tree
Who loves to lie with me,
And turn his merry note
Unto the sweet bird's throat,
Come hither, come hither, come hither;
Here shall he see
No enemy
But winter and rough weather.

Jaques. More, more, I prithee, more.

Ami. It will make you melancholy, Monsieur Jaques.

Jaq. I thank it. More, I prithee, more. I can suck melancholy out of a song, as a weasel sucks eggs. More, I prithee, more.

Ami. My voice is ragged: I know I cannot please you.

Jaq. I do not desire you to please me; I do desire you to sing. Come, more; another stanzo: call you 'em stanzos?

Ami. What you will, Monsieur Jaques.

Jaq. Nay, I care not for their names; they owe me nothing. Will you sing?

Ami. More at your request than to please myself.

Jaq. Well then, if ever I thank any man, I'll thank you; but that they call compliment is like the encounter of two dog-apes, and when a man thanks me heartily, methinks I have given him a penny and he renders me the beggarly thanks. Come, sing; and you that will not, hold your tongues.

Ami. Well, I'll end the song. Sirs, cover the while; the Duke will drink under this tree. He hath been all this day to look you.

Jaq. And I have been all this day to avoid him. He is too disputable for my company: I think of as many matters as he; but I give heaven thanks, and make no boast of them. Come, warble, come.

Ami.   Who doth ambition shun,
            And loves to live i' the sun,
            Seeking the food he eats,
            And pleased with what he gets,
       Come hither, come hither, come hither:
              Here shall he see
              No enemy
         But winter and rough weather.

Jaq. I'll give you a verse to this note, that I made yesterday in despite of my invention.

Ami. And I'll sing it.

Jaq. Thus it goes:
              If it do come to pass
              That any man turn ass,
            Leaving his wealth and ease
           A stubborn will to please,
      Ducdame, ducdame, ducdame:
              Here shall he see
             Gross fools as he,
         And if he will come to me.

Ami. What's that "ducdame"?

Jaq. 'Tis a Greek invocation, to call fools into a circle. I'll go sleep, if I can; if I cannot, I'll rail against all the first-born of Egypt.

Ami. And I'll go seek the Duke: his banquet is prepared.

                              As You Like It, Act II, Sc. V.

Henry Peacham

OF MUSICKE

MUSICKE A sister to Poetrie, next craveth your acquaintance (if your Genius be so disposed.) I know there are many, who are . . . of such disproportioned spirits, that they avoide her companie; as a great Cardinall in *Rome*, did Roses at their first coming in, that to avoide their scent, he built him an house in the champaigne farre from any towne: or as with a Rose so long since, a great Ladies cheeke in *England*, their eares are readie to blister at the tendrest touch thereof. I dare not passe so rash a censure of these as *Pindar* doth, or the *Italian*, having fitted a proverbe to the same effect, *Whom God loves not, that man loves not Musicke:* but I am very perswaded, they are by nature very ill disposed, and of such a brutish stupiditie, that scarce any thing else that is good and favoureth of vertue, is to be found in them. Never wise man (I thinke) questioned the lawfull use hereof, since it is an immediate gift of heaven, bestowed on man, whereby to praise and magnifie his Creator; to solace him in the midst of so many sorrowes and cares, wherewith life is hourely beset: and that by song, as by letters, the memorie of Doctrine, and the benefits of God might be for ever preferred (as we are taught by that Song of Moses, and those divine Psalmes of the sweet singer of Israel, who with his Psalterie so lowdly resounded the Mysteries and innumerable benefits of the Almightie Creator) and the service of God advanced, as we may find in 2 Samuel 6, vers. 5. Psalme 33.21.43 and 4.108.3, and in sundrie other places of Scripture which for brevitie I omit.

But, say our Sectaries, the service of God is nothing advanced by singing and instruments, as we use it in our Cathedral Churches, that is, by *Antiphonie, Restes, Repetitions, Varietie of Modes* and *Proportions* with the like.

For the first, that is not contrary, but consonant to the word of God, so in singing to answer either: the practise of Miriam the Prophetesse, and sister of Moses, when she answered the men in her song, will approve; For repetiton, nothing was more usual in the singing of the Levites, and among the Psalmes of David, the 136 is wholly compounded of those two most gracefull and sweete figures of repetition, *Symploce* and *Anaphora*.

For *Resting* and *Proportions*, the nature of the Hebrew verse, as the meanest Hebrician knoweth, consisting many times of uneven feete, going somtime in this number, sometimes in that; one while (as S. Hierome saith) in the numbers of Sappho;

another while of Alceus, doth of necessitie require it; and wherein doth our practise of singing and playing with Instruments in his Majesties Chappell, and our Cathedral Churches, differ from the practise of David, the Priests and Levites? *Doe we not make one sound in praising and thanking God, with Voyces and Instruments of all sorts? Donec* (as S. Hierome saith) *reboet laquear templi:* the roofe of the church echoeth againe, and which lest they should cavill at it as a Jewish Ceremonie, we know to have been practised in the ancient puritie of the Church; but we returne where we left.

The Physitians will tell you, that the exercise of Musicke is a great lengthener of the life, by stirring and reviving of the Spirits, holding a secret sympathy with them; Besides, the exercise of singing, openeth the breast and pipes; it is an enemy of melancholy and dejection of the mind, which S. Chrysostome truly calleth *The Devil's Bath.* Yea, a curer of some diseases: in Apuglie, in Italy, and thereabouts, it is moste certaine, that those who are stung by the Tarantula are cured only by Musicke. Beside the aforesaid benefit of singing, it is a most ready help for a bad pronunciation, and distinct speaking, which I have heard confirmed by many great Divines: yea, I my selfe have known many Children to have bin holpen of their stammering in speech, only by it.

Plato calleth it *A divine and heavenly practice*, profitable for the seeking out of that which is good and honest.

Homer saith, Musitians are worthy of Honor, and regard of the whole world; and we know, albeit Lycurgus imposeth most streight and sharp Lawes upon the Lacedaemonians, yet he ever allowed them the exercise of Musicke.

Aristotle averreth Musicke to be the only disposer of the mind to Vertue and Goodness; wherefore he reckoneth it among those foure principal exercises, wherein he would have children instructed. . . .

I might runne into an infinite Sea of the praise and use of so excellent an Art, but I onely shew it to you with the singer, because I desire not that any Noble or Gentleman should (save his private recreation at leisurable houres) proove a Master in the same, or neglect his more weightie imployments; though I avouch it a skill worthy of the knowledge and exercise of the greatest Prince.

King Henrie the eight could not onely sing his part sure, but of himselfe compose a Service of foure, five, and sixe parts; as Erasmus in a certaine Epistle testifieth of his owne knowledge.

But since the natural inclination of some men, driveth them (as it were) perforce to the top of Excellencie: examples of this kind are very rare, yea, great personages many times are more violently carried, then might well stand with their Honours, and necessitie of their affaires; yet were it to these honest and commendable exercises favouring of Vertue, it were well: but many neglecting their duties and places, will addict themselves wholly to trifles, and the most ridiculous and childish practices. As Eropus King of Macedonia, tooke pleasure only in making of Candles; Domitian, his recreation was to catch and kill flyes, and could not be spoken with many times in so serious an employment. Ptolomoeus Philadelphus was an excellent Smith and Basket Maker. Alphonso Atestivo Duke of Ferrara, delighted himselfe onely in turning and playing the Joiner. Rodolph the late Emperour in setting of Stones, and making Watches. Which and the like, much eclipse State and Majestie, bringing familiaritie, and by consequence contempt with the meanest.

I desire no more in you then to sing your part sure, and at the first sight, withall, to play the same upon your Violl, or the exercise of the Lute, privately to your selfe.

To deliver you an opinion, whom among other Authors you should imitate and allow for the best, there being so many equally good, is somewhat difficult; yet as in the rest herein you shall have my opinion.

For Motets, and Musicke of Pietie and Devotion, as well for the honour of our Nation, as the merit of the man, I preferre above all other our *Phoenix*, M. William Byrd, whom in that kind, I know not whether any man equall. I am sure, none excell, even by the judgement of France and Italy, who are very sparing of the commendation of strangers, in regard to that concept they hold of themselves. His *Cantiones Sacrae*, as also his *Gradualia*, are meere Angelicall and Divine; and being of himselfe naturally disposed to Gravitie and Pietie, his veine is not so much for light Madrigals or Canzonets, yet his *Virginella*, and some others of his first set, cannot be mended by the best Italian of them all.

I willingly, to avoid tediousness, forbeare to speake of the worth and excellency of the rest of our English Composers, Master Doctor Dowland, Thos. Morley, M. Alphonso, M. Wilbie, M. Kirbie, M. Wilkes, Michael East, M. Bateson, M. Deering, with sundry others, inferior to none in the world (how much soever the Italian attributes to himselfe) for depth of skill and richnesse of conceipt.

Infinite is the sweete varietie that the Theorique of Musicke exerciseth the mind withall, as the contemplation of proportions, of Concords and Discords, diversity of Moodes and Tones, infinitenesse of Invention, &c. But I dare affirme, there is no one Science in the world, that so affecteth the free and generous Spirit, with a more delightfull and in-offensive recreation, or better disposeth the minde to what is commendable and vertuous.

The Common-wealth of the Cynthenses, in Arcadia, falling from the delight they formerly had in Musicke, grew into seditious humours and civill warres, which Polybius tooke especially note of: and I suppose, heereupon it was ordained in Arcadia, that every one should practise Musicke by the space of thirty yeares.

The ancient Gauls in like manner (whom Julian tearmed barbarous) became most curteous and tractable by the practise of Musicke.

Yea, in my opinion, no Rhetoricke more perswadeth, or hath greater power over the mind; nay, hath not Musicke her figures, the same which (*sic*) Rhetorique? What is a *Revert* but her Antistrophe? her reports, but sweet *Anaphoras?* her counterchange of points, *Antimetaboles?* her passionate Aires but Prosopopoeas? with infinite other of the same nature.

How doth Musicke amaze us, when assures (*sic*) of discords she maketh the sweetest Harmony? And who can shew us the reason why two Basons, Bowles, Brasse Pots, or the like of the same bignesse; the one being full, the other emptie, shall, stricken, be a just *Diapason* in sound one to the other? or that there should bee such sympathy in sounds, that two Lutes of equal size being laid upon a Table, and tuned Unison, or alike in the Gamma, G sol re ut, or any other string; the one stricken, the other untouched shall answer it.

But to conclude, if all Arts hold their esteeme and value according to their Effects, account this goodly Science not among the number of those which Lucian placeth without the gates of Hell, as vaine and unprofitable; . . . since it is a principal meanes of glorying our mercifull Creator, it heightens our devotion, it gives delight and ease to our travailes, it expelleth sadnesse and heavinesse of Spirit, preserveth people in concord and amitie, allaieth fiercenesse and anger; and lastly, is the best Phisicke for many melancholy diseases.

The Compleat Gentleman, 1622, *Ch*. 11

Thomas Campian

DESCRIPTION OF A MASQUE

Presented before the King's Majesty at White Hall, on twelfth night last, in honour of the Lord Hayes and his bride, daughter and heir to the honourable the Lord Denny, their marriage having been the same day at Court solemnised.

AS IN battles, so in all other actions that are to be reported, the first, and most necessary part is the description of the place, with its opportunities and properties, whether they be natural or artificial. The great hall (wherein the Masque was presented) received this division, and order. The upper part where the cloth and chair of state were placed, had scaffolds and seats on either side continued to the screen; right before it was made a partition for the dancing-place; on the right hand whereof were consorted ten musicians, with bass and mean lutes[1] a bandora,[2] a double sackbut,[3] and an harpsichord, with two treble violins; on the other side somewhat nearer the screen were placed nine violins and three lutes, and to answer both the consorts (as it were in a triangle) six cornets, and six chapel voices, were seated almost right against them, in a place raised higher in respect of the piercing sound of those instruments; eighteen foot from the screen, another stage was raised higher by a yard than that which was prepared for dancing. This higher stage was all enclosed with a double veil, so artificially painted, that it seemed as if dark clouds had hung before it: within that shroud was concealed a green valley, with green trees round about it, and in the midst of them nine golden trees of fifteen foot high, with arms and branches very glorious to behold. From the which grove toward the stage was made a broad descent to the dancing place, just in the midst of it; on either side were two ascents, like the sides of two hills, drest with shrubs and trees; that on the right hand leading to the bower of Flora: the other to the house of Night; which bower and house were placed opposite at either end of the screen, and between them both was raised a hill, hanging like a cliff over the grove below, and on the top of it a goodly large tree was set, supposed to be the tree of Diana; behind the which toward the window was a small descent, with another spreading hill that climbed up to the top of the window, with many trees on the height of it, wherein those that played on the hautboys at the King's entrance into the hall were shadowed. The bower of Flora was very spacious, garnished with all kind of flowers, and flowery branches with lights in them; the house of Night ample and stately, with black pillars, whereon many stars of gold

[1] Alto or high tenor in compass.
[2] A bass cittern.
[3] Trombone.

39

were fixed: within it, when it was empty, appeared nothing but clouds and stars, and on the top of it stood three turrets under-propt with small starred pillars, the middlemost being highest and greatest, the other two of equal proportion: about it were placed on wire artificial bats and owls, continually moving; with many other inventions the which for brevity sake I pass by with silence.

Thus much for the place, and now from thence let us come to the persons.

The Masquers' names were these (whom both for order and honour I mention in the first place).

1. Lord Walden.
2. Sir Thomas Howard.
3. Sir Henry Carey, Master of the Jewel House.
4. Sir Richard Preston.
5. Sir John Ashley.   Gent. of the K. Privy Chamber.
6. Sir Thomas Jarret, Pensioner.
7. Sir John Digby, one of the King's Carvers.
8. Sir Thomas Badger, Master of the King's Harriers.
9. Master Goringe.

Their number nine, the best and amplest of numbers, for as in music seven notes contain all variety, the eight(h) being in nature the same as the first, so in numbering after the ninth we begin again, the tenth being as it were the diapason in arithmetic. The number of *nine* is framed by the Muses and Worthies, and it is of all the most apt for change and diversity of proportion. The chief habit which the Masquers did use is set forth to your view in the first leaf: they presented in their feigned persons the knights of Apollo, who is the father of heat and youth, and consequently of amorous affections.

The Speakers were in number four.

Flora, the queen of flowers, attired in a changeable taffeta gown, with a large veil embroidered with flowers, a crown of flowers, and white buskins painted with flowers.

Zephyrus, in a white loose robe of sky-coloured taffeta, with a mantle of white silk, propped with wire, still waving behind him as he moved; on his head he wore a wreath of palm deckt with primroses and violets, the hair of his head and beard were flaxen, and his buskins white, and painted with flowers.

Night, in a close robe of black silk and gold, a black mantle embroidered with stars, a crown of stars on her head, her hair black and spangled with gold, her face black, her buskins black, and painted with stars; in her hand she bore a black wand, wreathed with gold.

Hesperus, in a close robe of a deep crimson taffeta mingled with sky-colour, and over that a large loose robe of a lighter crimson taffeta; on his head he wore a wreathed band of gold, with a star in the front thereof, his hair and beard red, and buskins yellow.

These are the principal persons that bear sway in this invention, others that are but seconders to these, I will describe in their proper places, discoursing the Masque in order as it was performed.

As soon as the King was entered the great Hall, the Hoboys[1] (out of the wood on the top of the hill) entertained the time till his Majesty and his train were placed, and then after a little expectation the consort of ten began to play an air, at the sound whereof the veil on the right hand was withdrawn, and the ascent of the hill with the bower of Flora were discovered, where Flora and Zephyrus were busy plucking flowers from the bower, and throwing them into two baskets, which two Sylvans held, who were attired in changeable taffeta, with wreathes of flowers on their heads. As soon as the baskets were filled, they came down in this order; first Zephyrus and Flora, then the two Sylvans with baskets after them; four Sylvans in green taffeta and wreathes,

[1] Oboes.

41

two bearing mean lutes, the third, a bass lute, and the fourth a deep bandora.

As soon as they came to the descent toward the dancing place, the consort of ten ceased, and the four Sylvans played the same air, to which Zephyrus and the two other Sylvans did sing these words in a bass, tenor, and treble voice, and going up and down as they sung they strewed flowers all about the place.

SONG

Now hath Flora robbed her bowers
To befriend this place with flowers:
    Strow about, strow about!
The sky rained never kindlier showers.
Flowers with bridals well agree,
Fresh as brides and bridegrooms be:
    Strow about, strow about!
And mix them with fit melody.
Earth hath no princelier flowers
Than roses white and roses red,
But they must still be mingled:
And as the rose new plucked from Venus' thorn,
So doth a bride her bridegroom's bed adorn.

Divers divers flowers affect
For some private dear respect:
    Strow about, strow about!
Let every one his own protect;
But he's none of Flora's friend
That will not the rose commend.
    Strow about, strow about!
Let princes princely flowers defend:
Roses, the garden's pride,
Are flowers for love and flowers for kings,
In courts desired and weddings:
And as a rose in Venus' bosom worn,
So doth a bridegroom his bride's bed adorn.

The music ceaseth and Flora speaks.

This spoken, the four Sylvans played on their instruments
the first strain of this song following: and at the repetition thereof
the voices fell in with the instruments which were thus divided:
a treble and a bass were placed near his Majesty, and another
treble and bass near the grove, that the words of the song might
be heard of all, because the trees of gold instantly at the first
sound of their voices began to move and dance according to
the measure of the time which the musicians kept in singing, and
the nature of the words which they delivered.

SONG

Move now with measured sound,
You charmed grove of gold,
Trace forth the sacred ground
That shall your forms unfold.

Diana and the starry Night for your Apollo's sake
Endue your Sylvan shapes with power this strange delight to make.
Much joy must needs the place betide where trees for gladness
move:
A fairer sight was ne'er beheld, or more expressing love.

Yet nearer Phoebus' throne
Meet on your winding ways,
Your bridal mirth make known
In your high-graced Hayes.

Let Hymen lead your sliding rounds, and guide them with his
light,
While we do Io Hymen sing in honour of this night,
Join three by three, for so the night by triple spell decrees,
Now to release Apollo's knights from these enchanted trees.

This dancing-song being ended, the golden trees stood in ranks three by three, and Night ascended up to the grove, and spake thus, touching the first three severally with her wand.

Night.   By virtue of this wand, and touch divine,
These Sylvan shadows back to earth resign:
Your native forms resume, with habit fair,
While solemn music shall enchant the air.

Presently the Sylvans with their four instruments, and five voices, began to play, and sing together the song following; at the beginning whereof that part of the stage whereon the first three trees stood began to yield, and the three foremost trees gently to sink, and this was effected by an engine placed under the stage.[1] When the trees had sunk a yard they cleft in three parts, and the Masquers appeared out of the tops of them, the trees were suddenly conveyed away, and the first three Masquers were raised again by the engine. They appeared then in a false habit, yet very fair, and in form not much unlike their principal and true robe. It was made of green taffeta cut into leaves, and laid upon cloth of silver, and their hats were suitable to the same.

SONG OF TRANSFORMATION

Night and Diana charge,
        And th'Earth obeys,
Opening large
        Her secret ways,
While Apollo's charmed men
        Their forms receive again.
Give gracious Phoebus honour then,
And so fall down, and rest behind the train,
Give gracious Phoebus honour then,
And so fall, &c.

---

[1] Inigo Jones's machine would only accommodate three men, so the nine Masquers had to appear three at a time.

When these words were sung, the three Masquers made an honour to the King, and so falling back the other six trees, three by three, came forward, and when they were in their appointed places, Night spake again thus:

Night. Thus can celestials work in human fate,
Transform and form as they do love or hate;
Like touch and change receive. The Gods agree:
The best of numbers is contained in three.

THE SONG OF TRANSFORMATION AGAIN

Night and Diana, &c.

Then Night touched the second three trees and the stage sunk with them as before: and in brief the second three did in all points as the first. Then Night spake again.

Night. The last, and third of nine, touch, magic wand,
And give them back their forms at Night's command.

Night touched the third three trees, and the same charm of Night and Diana was sung the third time; the last three trees were transformed, and the Masquers raised, when presently the first Music began his full Chorus.

Again this song receive and sound on high:
Long live Apollo, Britain's glorious eye!

This chorus was in manner of an Echo, seconded by the cornets, then by the consort of ten, then by the consort of twelve, and by the double chorus of voices standing on either side, the one against the other, bearing five voices apiece, and sometime every chorus was heard severally, sometime mixed, but in the end all together: which kind of harmony so distinguished by the place, and by the several nature of the instruments, and changeable conveyance of

the song, and performed by so many excellent masters as were
actors in that music, (the number in all amounting to forty two
voices and instruments) could not but yield great satisfaction to
the hearers.

While this chorus was repeated twice over, the nine masters
in their green habits solemnly descended to the dancing-place,
in such order as they were to begin their dance, and as soon as
the chorus ended, the violins, or consort of twelve began to play
the second new dance, which was taken in form of an echo by the
cornets, and then catched in like manner by the consort of ten,
(sometime they mingled two musics together; sometime played
all at once;) which kind of echoing music rarely became their
Sylvan attire, and was so truly mixed together, that no dance
could ever be better graced than that, as (in such distraction of
music) it was performed by the Masquers. After this dance Night
descended from the grove, and addressed her speech to the
masquers, as followeth.

Night. Phoebus is pleased, and all rejoice to see
His servants from their golden prison free.
But yet since Cynthia hath so friendly smiled,
And to you tree-born knights is reconciled,
First ere you any more work undertake,
About her tree solemn procession make,
  Diana's tree, the tree of Chastity,
That placed alone on yonder hill you see.
These green-leaved robes, wherein disguised you made
Stealths to her nymphs through the thick forest's shade,
There to the goddess offer thankfully,
That she may not in vain appeased be.
The Night shall guide you, and her Hours attend you
That no ill eyes, or spirits shall offend you.

At the end of this speech Night began to lead the way alone,
and after her an Hour with his torch, after the Hour was a

46

masquer; and so in order one by one, a torch-bearer and a
masquer, they march on towards Diana's tree. When the
masquers came by the house of Night, every one by his Hour
received his helmet, and had his false robe plucked off, and,
bearing it in his hand, with a low honour offered it at the tree
of Chastity, and so in his glorious habit, with his Hour before
him, marched to the bower of Flora. The shape of their habit
the picture before discovers, the stuff was of carnation satin laid
thick with broad silver lace, their helmets being made of the
same stuff. So through the bower of Flora they came, where
they joined two torch-bearers and two masquers, and when they
past down the grove, the Hours parted on either side, and made
way between them for the masquers, who descended to the
dancing-place in such order as they were to begin their third
new dance. All this time of procession the six cornets, and six
chapel voices sung a solemn motet of six parts made upon these
words.

> With spotless minds now mount we to the tree
> > Of single chastity.
> The root is temperance grounded deep,
> Which the cold-juiced earth doth steep:
> > Water it desires alone,
> > Other drink it thirsts for none:
> Therewith the sober branches it doth feed,
> > Which though they faultless be,
> Yet comely leaves they breed,
> > To beautify the tree.
> Cynthia protectress is, and for her sake
> We this grave procession make.
> Chaste eyes and ears, pure hearts and voices,
> Are graces wherein Phoebe most rejoices.

The motet being ended, the violins began the third new dance,
which was lively performed by the masquers, after which they
took forth the ladies, and danced the measures with them; which

being finished, the masquers brought the ladies back again to their places.

Sir Francis Bacon

OF MASQUES AND TRIUMPHS

THESE THINGS are but toys, to come amongst such serious observations. But yet, since princes will have such things, it is better they should be graced with elegancy, than daubed with cost. Dancing to song is a thing of great state and pleasure. I understand it, that the song be in quire, placed aloft, and accompanied with some broken music;[1] and the ditty fitted to the device. Acting in song, especially in dialogues, hath an extreme good grace: I say acting, not dancing (for that is a mean and vulgar thing); and the voices of the dialogue should be strong and manly (a bass and a tenor, no treble); and the ditty high and tragical, not nice or dainty. Several quires, placed one over against another, and taking the voice by catches, anthem-wise, give great pleasure. Turning dances into figure is a childish curiosity. And generally, let it be noted, that those things which I here set down are such as do naturally take the sense, and not respect petty wonderments. It is true, the alterations of scenes, so it be quietly and without noise, are things of great beauty and pleasure; for they feed and relieve the eye, before it be full of the same object. Let the scenes abound with light, specially coloured and varied; and let the masquers, or any other, that are to come down from the scene, have some motions upon the scene itself before their coming down; for it draws the eye strangely, and makes it with great pleasure to desire to see that it cannot perfectly discern. Let the songs be loud and cheerful, and not chirpings or pulings. Let the music likewise be sharp and loud and well placed. The colours that show best by candle-light are white, carnation, and a kind of sea-water-green; and oes,[2] or spangs, as they are of no great cost, so they are of most

---

[1] Music by a broken consort, i.e., a mixed ensemble of instruments.

[2] Sequins.

glory. As for rich embroidery, it is lost and not discerned. Let the suits of the masquers be graceful, and such as become the person when the visars are off: not after examples of known attires; Turks, soldiers, mariners, and the like. Let antimasques not be long; they have been commonly of fools, satyrs, baboons, wild-men, antics, beasts, sprites, witches, Ethiopes, pigmies, turquets, nymphs, rustics, Cupids, statuas moving, and the like. As for angels, it is not comical enough to put them in anti-masques; and any thing that is hideous, as devils, giants, is on the other side as unfit. But chiefly, let the music of them be recreative, and with some strange changes. Some sweet odours, suddenly coming forth, without any drops falling, are, in such a company as there is steam and heat, things of great pleasure and refreshment. Double masques, one of men, another of ladies, addeth state and variety. But all is nothing, except the room be kept clear and neat.

For justs, and tourneys, and barriers; the glories of them are chiefly in the chariots, wherein the challengers make their entry; especially if they be drawn with strange beasts, as lions, bears, camels, and the like; or in the devices of their entrance; or in the bravery of their liveries; or in the goodly furniture of their horses and armour. But enough of these toys.

Essays

Ben Jonson

COMMON THEFT TO MUSIC

Scene: An old English Fair.
Booths and Stalls with their attendants.
Present on the Stage:
        Bartholomew Cokes; an Esquire of Harrow.
        Humphrey Waspe; His Man.
        Winwife; his Rival.
        Tom Quarlous; Winwife's companion, a gamester.

Mrs. Overdo; wife of Adam Overdo.

Grace; their ward.

Enter: Ezechiel Edgeworth, a Cutpurse. Nightingale, a Ballad-singer, followed at a distance by Adam Overdo, a Justice of the Peace, disguised.

Over. I cannot beget a project, with all my political brain yet: my project is how to fetch off this proper young man from his debauched company. I have followed him all the Fair over, and still I find him with this songster, and I begin shrewdly to suspect their familiarity; and the young man of a terrible taint, poetry! with which idle disease if he be infected, there's no hope of him, in a state-course. *Actum est* of him for a commonwealth's-man, if he go to't in rhyme once. (*Aside.*

Edg. (to Nightingale). Yonder he is buying of gingerbread; set in quickly, before he part with too much of his money.

Night. (advancing and singing). My masters, and friends, and good people, draw near—

Cokes. (runs to the ballad-man). Ballads! hark! hark! pray thee, fellow, stay a little; good Numps, look to the goods. What ballads hast thou? let me see, let me see myself.

Waspe. Why so! he's flown to another lime-bush, there he will flutter as long more; till he have ne'er a feather left. Is there a vexation like this, gentlemen? will you believe me now, hereafter, shall I have credit with you?

Quar. Yes, faith shalt thou, Numps, and thou art worthy on't, for thou sweatest for't. I never saw a young pimp-errant and his squire better match'd.

Winw. Faith, the sister comes after them well too.

Grace. Nay, if you saw the justice her husband, my guardian, you were fitted for the mess, he is such a wise one his way—

Winw. I wonder we see him not here.

Grace. Oh! he is too serious for this place, and yet better sport then than the other three, I assure you, gentlemen, wherever he is, though it be on the bench.

Cokes. How dost thou call it? *A caveat against cut-purses!* a good jest, i'faith, I would fain see that demon, your cut-purse you talk of, that delicate-handed devil; they say he walks hereabout: I would see him walk now. Look you, sister, here, here, (*he shows his purse boastingly*) let him come, sister, and welcome. Ballad-man, does any cut-purses haunt hereabout? pray thee raise me one or two; begin, and shew me one.

Night. Sir, this is a spell against them, spick and span new; and 'tis made as 'twer in mine own person, and I sing it in mine own defence. But 'twill cost a penny alone, if you buy it.

Cokes. No matter for the price; thou dost not know me, I see, I am an old Bartholomew.

Mrs. Over. Has it a fine picture, brother?

Cokes. O, sister, do you remember the ballads over the nursery chimney at home o' my own pasting up? there be brave pictures, other manner of pictures than these, friend.

Waspe. Yet these will serve to pick the pictures out of your pockets, you shall see.

Cokes. So I heard them say! Pray thee mind him not, fellow; he'll have an oar in every thing.

Night. It was intended, sir, as if a purse should chance to be cut in my presence, now, I may be blameless though: as by the sequel will more plainly appear.

Cokes. We shall find that in the matter: pray thee begin.

Night. To the tune of *Paggington's Pound*, sir.

Cokes. (*sings*). Fa, la la, la la la, fa, la la la la! Nay, I'll put thee in tune and all; mine own country dance! Pray thee begin.

Night. It is a gentle admonition, you must know, sir, both to the purse-cutter and the purse-bearer.

Cokes. Not a word more out of the tune, an thou lov'st me; Fa, la, la la, la la la, fa, la la la. Come, when?

Night. (*sings*)

My masters, and friends, and good people, draw near,
    And look to your purses, for that I do say;

Cokes. Ha, ha, this chimes! Good counsel at first dash.

Night. And tho' little money in them you do bear,
    It costs more to get, than to lose in a day.

Cokes. Good!

Night.   You oft have been told,
                    Both the young and the old,
             And bidden beware of the cut-purse so bold;

Cokes. Well said! he were to blame that would not, i'faith.

Night. Then if you take heed not, free me from the curse,
             Who both give you warning, for, and the cut-purse.
             Youth, youth, thou had'st better been starv'd by thy
                                                                    nurse,
             Than live to be hanged for cutting a purse.

Cokes. Good, i'faith; how say you, Numps, is there any harm
    in this?

Night. It hath been upbraided to men of my trade,
             That oftentimes we are the cause of this crime;

Cokes. The more coxcombs they that did it, I wusse.

Night. Alack and for pity, why should it be said?
             As if they regarded or places or time!
                    Examples have been
                    Of some that were seen
             In Westminster-hall, yea, the pleaders between;
             Then why should the judges be free from this curse,
             More than my poor self, for cutting the purse?

Cokes. God a mercy for that! why should they be more free
    indeed?

Night. Youth, youth, thou had'st better been starv'd by thy
                                                                    nurse,
             Than live to be hanged for cutting a purse.

Cokes. That again, good ballad-man, that again. (*He sings the
    burden with him*) O rare! I would fain rub mine elbow, now,
    but I dare not pull out my hand.—On I pray thee; he that made
    this ballad shall be poet to my masque.

Night. At Worc'ster, 'tis known well, and even in the jail,
                    A knight of good worship did there show his face,
             Against the foul sinners, in zeal for to rail,
                    And lost *ipso facto* his purse in the place.

Cokes. Is it possible?

Night.   Nay, once from the seat
        Of judgment so great,
    A judge there did lose a fair pouch of velvète.

Cokes. I'faith?

Night. O Lord for thy mercy, how wicked or worse,
    Are those that so venture their necks for a purse!
    Youth, youth, thou had'st better been starv'd by thy
                           nurse,
    Than live to be hanged for cutting a purse.

Cokes (sings after him).
        Youth, youth thou had'st better etc.
Pray thee, stay a little, friend. Yet o' thy conscience, Numps,
speak, is there any harm in this?

Waspe. To tell you true, 'tis too good for you, less you had
grace to follow it.

Over. It doth discover enormity, I'll mark it more: I have not
liked a paltry piece of poetry so well a good while.   (*Aside*

Cokes.   Youth, youth, etc.;
Where's this fellow now? a man must call upon him for his
own good, and yet he will not appear. Look here, here's for
him; (*shews his purse*) handy dandy, which hand will he have?
On, I pray thee, with the rest; I do hear of him, but I cannot
see him, this master youth, the cut-purse.

Night. At plays, and at sermons, and at the sessions,
    'Tis daily their practice such booty to make.
    Yea under the gallows at executions,
    They stick not the stare-abouts' purses to take.
        Nay one without grace,
        At a much better place,
    At Court, and at Christmas, before the king's face.

Cokes. That was a fine fellow! I would have him now.

Night. Alack then for pity must I bear the curse,
    That only belongs to the cunning cut-purse?

Cokes. But where's their cunning now, when they should use
it? they are all chain'd now, I warrant you. (*sings*)
    Youth, youth, thou had'st better—

The rat-catchers' charms are all fools and asses to this: a pox
on them, that they will not come! that a man should have a
desire to a thing, and want it!

Quar. 'Fore God I'd give half the Fair, an 'twere mine, for a
cut-purse for him, to save his longing.

Cokes. Look you, sister (shews his purse again), here, here,
where is't now? which pocket is't in, for a wager?

Waspe. I beseech you leave your wagers, and let him end his
matter, an't may be.

Cokes. O, are you edified, Numps!

Over. Indeed he does interrupt him too much: there Numps
spoke to purpose. *(Aside*

Cokes. Sister, I am an ass, I cannot keep my purse! (*Shews it
again, and puts it up*)—On, on, I pray thee, friend.

Night. Youth, youth, thou had'st better been starv'd by thy
nurse,

Than live to be hanged for cutting a purse.

(*As Nightingale sings, Edgeworth gets up to Cokes, and tickles him
in the ear with a straw twice to draw his hand out of his pocket*).

Winw. Will you see sport? look, there's a fellow gathers up
to him, mark.

Quar. Good, i'faith! O he has lighted on the wrong pocket.

Winw. He has it! 'for God, he is a brave fellow: pity he should
be detected.

Night. But O, you vile nation of cut-purses all,

Relent and repent, and amend and be sound,

And know that you ought not, by honest men's fall,

Advance your own fortunes, to die above ground;

And though you go gay

In silks, as you may,

It is not the highway to heaven (as they say).

Repent then, repent you, for better, for worse,

And kiss not the gallows for cutting a purse,

Youth, youth, thou had'st better been starv'd by thy nurse,

Than live to be hanged for cutting a purse.

All. An excellent ballad! an excellent ballad!

Edg. Friend, let me have the first, let me have the first, I pray you.

(*As Nightingale reaches out the ballad, Edgeworth slips the purse into his hand.*)

Cokes. Pardon me, sir; first come first served; and I'll buy the whole bundle, too.

Winw. That conveyance was better than all, did you see't? he has given the purse to the ballad-singer.

Quar. Has he?

Edg. Sir, I cry you mercy, I'll not hinder the poor man's profit; pray you, mistake me not.

Cokes. Sir, I take you for an honest gentleman, if that be mistaking; I met you to-day afore: ha! humph! O Lord! my purse is gone, my purse, my purse, my purse!

Waspe. Come do not make a stir, and cry yourself an ass thorough the Fair afore your time.

Cokes. Why, hast thou it, Numps? good Numps, how came you by it, I marle?

Waspe. I pray you seek some other gamester to play the fool with; you may lose it time enough, for all your Fair wit.

Cokes. By this good hand, glove and all, I have lost it already if thou hast it not; feel else, and mistress Grace's handkerchief too, out of t'other pocket.

Waspe. Why, 'tis well, very well, exceeding pretty and well.

Edg. Are you sure you have lost it, sir?

Cokes. O Lord! yes; as I am an honest man, I had it but e'en now at "Youth, youth."

Night. I hope you suspect not me, sir?

Edg. Thee! that were a jest indeed! dost thou think the gentleman is foolish? where had'st thou hands, I pray thee? Away, ass, away! (*Exit Night*

Over. I shall be beaten again, if I be spied. (*Aside retiring.*

Edg. Sir, I suspect an odd fellow, yonder, is stealing away.

Mrs. Over. Brother, it is the preaching fellow: you shall suspect him. He was at your t'other purse, you know! (*Seizes Overdo*) —Nay, stay, sir, and view the work you have done; an you be

55

beneficed at the gallows, and preach there, thank your own handywork.

Cokes. Sir, you shall take no pride in your preferment, you shall be silenced quickly.   (*They seize Overdo*

Over. What do you mean, sweet buds of gentility?

Cokes. To have my pennyworths out of you, bud. No less than two purses a day serve you! I thought you a simple fellow, when my man Numps beat you in the morning, and pitied you.

Mrs. Over. So did I, I'll be sworn, brother; but now I see he is a lewd and pernicious enormity, as master Overdo calls him.

Over. Mine own words turned upon me like swords!   (*Aside*

Cokes. Cannot a man's purse be at quiet for you in the master's pocket, but you must entice it forth, and debauch it?

    (*Overdo is carried off*

Waspe. Sir, sir, keep your debauch, and your fine Bartholomew terms to yourself, and make as much on 'em as you please. But give me this from you in the mean time; I beseech you, see if I can look to this.

Cokes. Why, Numps?

Waspe. Why! because you are an ass, sir, there's a reason the shortest way, an you will needs have it: now you have got the trick of losing, you'd lose your breech an 'twer loose. I know you, sir, come, deliver (*takes the box from him*), you'll go and crack the vermin you breed now, will you? 'tis very fine; will you have the truth on't? they are such retchless flies as you are, that blow cut-purses abroad in every corner; your foolish having of money makes them. An there were no wiser than I, sir, the trade should lie open for you, sir, it should, i'faith, sir, as well as your land to come into your hand, I assure you, sir.

Winw. Alack, good Numps!

Waspe. Nay, gentlemen, never pity me, I am not worth it: Lord send me at home once to Harrow o' the Hill, again, if I travel any more, call me Coriat with all my heart.

    (*Exeunt*

Bartholomew Fair, Act II

The English Bible, Authorised Version

SAUL AND DAVID

BUT THE spirit of the Lord departed from Saul, and an evil spirit from the Lord troubled him.

And Saul's servants said unto him, Behold now, an evil spirit from God troubleth thee.

Let our lord now command thy servants, which are before thee, to seek out a man, who is a cunning player on an harp: and it shall come to pass, when the evil spirit from God is upon thee, that he shall play with his hand, and thou shalt be well.

And Saul said unto his servants, Provide me now a man that can play well, and bring him to me.

Then answered one of the servants, and said, Behold, I have seen a son of Jesse the Beth-lehemite, that is cunning in playing, and a mighty valiant man, and a man of war, and prudent in matters, and a comely person, and the Lord is with him.

Wherefore Saul sent messengers unto Jesse, and said, Send me David thy son, which is with the sheep.

And Jesse took an ass laden with bread, and a bottle of wine, and a kid, and sent them by David his son unto Saul.

And David came to Saul, and stood before him: and he loved him greatly; and he became his armourbearer.

And Saul sent to Jesse, saying, Let David, I pray thee, stand before me; for he hath found favour in my sight.

And it came to pass, when the evil spirit from God was upon Saul, that David took an harp, and played with his hand: so Saul was refreshed, and was well, and the evil spirit departed from him.

And David went out withersoever Saul sent him, and behaved himself wisely: and Saul set him over the men of war, and he was accepted in the sight of all the people, and also in the sight of Saul's servants.

And it came to pass as they came, when David was returned from the slaughter of the Philistine, that the women came out of all cities of Israel, singing and dancing, to meet king Saul, with tabrets, with joy, and with instruments of musick.

And the women answered one another as they played, and said, Saul hath slain his thousands, and David his ten thousands.

And Saul was very wroth, and the saying displeased him; and he said, They have ascribed unto David ten thousands, and to me they have ascribed but thousands: and what can he have more but the kingdom?

And Saul eyed David from that day and forward.

And it came to pass on the morrow, that the evil spirit from God came upon Saul, and he prophesied in the midst of the house: and David played with his hand, as at other times: and there was a javelin in Saul's hand.

And Saul cast the javelin; for he said, I will smite David even to the wall with it. And David avoided out of his presence twice.

And Saul was afraid of David, because the Lord was with him and was departed from Saul.

I Samuel, Ch. XVI, v. 14-23: Ch. XVIII, v. 5-12

Izaak Walton

FROM THE LIFE OF GEORGE HERBERT

HIS CHIEFEST recreation was music, in which heavenly art he was a most excellent master, and did himself compose many divine hymns and anthems, which he set and sung to his lute or viol; and though he was a lover of retiredness, yet his love of music was such, that he went usually twice every week, on certain appointed days to the cathedral church in Salisbury; and at his return would say, that his time spent in prayer and cathedral music elevated his soul, and was his heaven upon earth. But before his return thence to Bemerton, he would usually sing and play his part at an appointed private music meeting; and, to justify this practice, he would often say, religion does not banish mirth, but only moderates and sets rules to it.

And as his desire to enjoy his heaven upon earth drew him twice every week to Salisbury, so his walks thither were the occasion of many happy accidents to others, of which I will mention some few.

In one of his walks to Salisbury, he overtook a gentleman that is still living in that city, and in their walk together Mr. Herbert took a fair occasion to talk with him, and humbly begged to be excused if he asked him some account of his faith; and said, "I do this the rather because though you are not of my parish, yet I receive tithe from you by the hand of your tenant; and, sir, I am the bolder to do it, because I know there be some sermon hearers that be like those fishes that always live in salt water, and yet are always fresh." After which expression Mr. Herbert asked him some needful questions, and having received his answer, gave him such rules for the trial of his sincerity, and for a practical piety, and in so loving and meek a manner, that the gentleman did so fall in love with him and his discourse, that he would often contrive to meet him in his walk to Salisbury, or to attend him back to Bemerton, and still mentions the name of Mr. George Herbert with veneration, and still praiseth God for the occasion of knowing him.

In another walk to Salisbury he saw a poor man with a poorer horse that had fallen under his load; they were both in distress, and needed present help, which Mr. Herbert perceiving, put off his canonical coat, and helped the poor man to unload, and after to load his horse. The poor man blessed him for it, and he blessed the poor man; and was so like the good Samaritan, that he gave him money to refresh both himself and his horse, and told him, that if he loved himself, he should be merciful to his beast. Thus he left the poor man, and at his coming to his musical friends at Salisbury, they began to wonder that Mr. George Herbert, who used to be so trim and clean, came into that company so soiled and discomposed; but he told them the occasion; and when one of the company told him he had disparaged himself by so dirty an employment, his answer was, that the thought of what he had done would prove music to him at midnight, and that the omission of it would have upbraided him and made discord in his conscience, whensoever he should pass by that place. "For if I be bound to pray for all that be in distress. I am sure that I am bound, so far as it is in my power, to practice what I pray for. And though I do not wish for the like occasion every day, yet let me tell you, I would not willingly pass one day of my life without comforting a sad soul, or showing mercy; and I praise God for this occasion. And now let us tune our instruments."

The Life of Mr. George Herbert

Robert Burton

THE FOOD OF LOVE

'TIS THE humour of all suitors to trick up themselves, to be prodigal in apparel, *purè lotus*, neat, combed, and curled, with powdered hair, *comptus et calamistratus*, with a long love-lock, a flower in his ear, perfumed gloves, rings, scarfs, feathers, points, &c. as if he were a prince's Ganymede, with every day new suits, as the fashion varies; going as if he trod upon eggs, and as Heinsius writ to Primierus, "if once he be besotten on a wench, he must lie awake at nights, renounce his book, sigh and lament, now and then weep for his hard hap, and mark above all things what hats, bands, doublets, breeches, are in fashion, how to cut his beard, and wear his locks, to turn up his mustachios, and curl his head, prune his pickitivant, or if he wear it abroad, that the east side be correspondent to the west:" he may be scoffed at otherwise, as Julian that apostate was for wearing a long hirsute goatish beard, fit to make ropes with, as in his Mysopogone, or that apologetical oration he made at Antioch to excuse himself, he doth ironically confess, it hindered his kissing, *nam non licuit inde pura puris, eoque suavioribus labra labris adjungere*, but he did not much esteem it, as it seems by the sequel, *de accipiendis dandisve osculis non laboro*, yet (to follow mine authority) it may much concern a young lover, he must be more respectful in his behalf, "he must be in league with an excellent tailor, barber",

"*i Tonsorem puerum sed arte talem,*
Qualis nec Thalamis fuit Neronis;"

"have neat shoe-ties, points, garters, speak in print, walk in print, eat and drink in print, and that which is all in all, he must be mad in print."

Amongst other good qualities an amorous fellow is endowed with, he must learn to sing and dance, play upon some instrument or other, as without all doubt he will, if he be truly touched with this loadstone of love. For as Erasmus hath it, *Musicam docet amro et Poesin*, love will make them musicians, and to compose ditties, madrigals, elegies, love sonnets, and sing them to several pretty tunes, to get all good qualities may be had. Jupiter perceived Mercury to be in love with Philologia, because he learned languages, polite speech (for Suadela herself was Venus' daughter as some write), arts and sciences, *Quo virgini placeret*, all to ingratiate himself, and please his mistress. 'Tis their chiefest study to sing, dance; and without question, so many gentlemen and gentlewomen would not be so well qualified in this kind, if love did not incite them. "Who", saith Castilio, "would learn to play, or give his mind to music, learn to dance, or make so many rhymes, lovesongs, as most do, but for women's sake, because they hope by that means to purchase their good wills, and win their favour?" We see this daily verified in our young women and wives, they that being maids took so much pains to sing, play, and dance, with such cost and charge to their parents, to get those graceful qualities, now being married will scarce touch an instrument, they care not for it. Constantine *agricult. lib.* 11. *cap.* 18, makes Cupid himself to be a great dancer; by the same token that he was capering amongst the gods, "he flung down a bowl of nectar, which distilling upon the white rose, ever since made it red:" and Calistratus, by the help of Daedalus, about Cupid's statue made a many of young wenches still a dancing, to signify belike that Cupid was much affected with it, as without all doubt he was. For at his and Psyche's wedding, the gods being present to grace the feast, Ganymede filled nectar in abundance (as Apuleius describes it), Vulcan was the cook, the Hours made all fine with music and flowers, Apollo played on the harp, the Muses sang to it, *sed suavi Musicæ super ingressa Venus saltavit*, but his mother Venus danced to his and their sweet content. Witty Lucian in that pathetical love passage, or pleasant description of Jupiter's stealing of Europa, and swimming from Phoenicia to Crete, makes the sea calm, the winds hush, Neptune and Amphitrite riding in their chariot to break the waves before them, the tritons dancing round about, with every one a torch, the sea-nymphs half-naked, keeping time on dolphins' backs, and singing Hymeneus, Cupid nimbly tripping on the top of the waters, and Venus herself coming after in a shell, strewing roses and flowers on their heads. Praxiteles, in all his pictures of love, feigns Cupid ever smiling, and looking upon dancers; and in Saint Mark's in Rome (whose work I know not), one of the most delicious pieces, is a many of Satyrs dancing about a wench asleep. So that dancing still is as it were a necessary appendix to love matters. Young lasses are never better pleased than when as upon a holiday, after evensong, they may meet their sweethearts, and dance about a maypole, or in a town-green under a shady elm. Nothing so familiar in France, as for citizens' wives and maids to dance a round in the streets, and often too, for want of better instruments, to make good music of their own voices, and dance after it. Yea many times this love will make old men and women that have more toes than teeth, dance,—"John, come kiss me now", mask and mum; for Comus and Hymen love masks, and all such merriments above measure, will allow men to put on women's apparel in some cases, and promiscuously to dance, young and old, rich and poor, generous and base, of all sorts. Paulus Jovius taxeth Augustine Niphus the philosopher, "for that being an old man and a public professor, a father of many children, he was so mad for the love of a young maid (that which many of his friends were ashamed to see), an old gouty fellow, yet would dance after fiddlers." Many laughed him to scorn for it, but this omnipotent love would have it so.

"*Hyacinthino bacillo* *Properans amor, me adegit* *Violenter ad sequendum.*"	"Love hasty with his purple staff did make Me follow and the dance to undertake."

And 'tis no news this, no indecorum; for why? a good reason may be given of it. Cupid and death meet both in an inn; and being merrily disposed, they did exchange arrows from either quiver; ever since young men die, and oftentimes old men dote— *Sic moritur Juvenis, sic moribundus amat.* And who can then withstand it? If once we be in love, young or old, though our teeth shake in our heads like virginal jacks, or stand parallel asunder like the arches of a bridge, there is no remedy, we must dance trenchmore for a need, over tables, chairs, and stools, &c. And Princum Prancum is a fine dance. Plutarch, *Sympos.* 1. *quæ st.* 5. doth in some sort excuse it, and telleth us moreover in what sense, *Musicam docet amor, licet prius fuerit rudis,* how love makes them that had no skill before learn to sing and dance; he concludes, 'tis only that power and prerogative love hath over us. "Love (as he holds) will make a silent man speak, a modest man officious; dull, quick; slow, nimble; and that which is most to be admired, a hard, base, untractable churl, as fire doth iron in a smith's forge, free, facile, gentle and easy to be entreated." Nay, 'twill make him prodigal in the other extreme, and give a hundred sesterces for a night's lodging, as they did of old to Lais of Corinth, or *ducenta drachmarum millia pro unica nocte,* as Mundus to Paulina, spend all his fortunes (as too many do in like case) to obtain his suit. For which cause many compare love to wine, which makes men jovial and merry, frolic and sad, whine, sing, dance, and what not.

But above all the other symptoms of lovers, this is not lightly to be overpassed, that likely of what condition soever, if once they be in love, they turn to their ability, rhymers, ballad-makers and poets. For as Plutarch saith, "They will be witnesses and trumpeters of their paramours' good parts, bedecking them with verses and commendatory songs, as we do statues with gold, that they may be remembered and admired of all." Ancient men will dote in this kind sometimes as well as the rest; the heat of love will thaw their frozen affections, dissolve the ice of age, and so far enable them, though they be sixty years of age above the girdle, to be scarce thirty beneath. Jovianus Pontanus makes an old fool rhyme, and turn Poetaster to please his mistress.

"*Me ringas Mariana, meos*	"Sweet Marian do not mine
ne despice canos,	age disdain,
Desene nam juvenem dia	For thou canst make an old
referre potes," &c.	man young again."

They will be singing amorous songs and ditties (if young especially), and cannot abstain though it be when they go to, or should be at church. We have a pretty story to this purpose in Westmonasteriensis an old writer of ours (if you will believe it) An. Dom. 1012 at Colewiz in Saxony, on Christmas eve a company of young men and maids, whilst the priest was at mass in the church, were singing catches and love songs in the church-yard, he sent to them to make less noise, but they sung on still: and if you will, you shall have the very song itself.

"*Equitabat homo per sylvam*	"A fellow rid by the
frondosam,	greenwood side,
Ducebatque secum Meswinden	And fair Meswinde was his
formosam,	bride,
Quid stamus, cur non	Why stand we so, and
imus?"	do not go?"

This they sung, he chaft, till at length, impatient as he was, he prayed to St. Magnus, patron of the church, they might all three sing and dance till that time twelvemonth, and so they did without meat and drink, wearisomeness or giving over, till at year's end they ceased singing, and were absolved by Herebertus

Archbishop of Cologne. They will in all places be doing thus, young folks especially, reading love stories, talking of this or that young man, such a fair maid, singing, telling or hearing lascivious tales, scurrilous tunes, such objects are their sole delight, their continual meditation, and as Guastavinius adds, *Com. in 4. Sect. 27. Prov. Arist. ob seminis abundatiam crebræ cogitationes, veneris frequens recordatio et pruriens voluptas,* &c. an earnest longing comes hence, *pruriens corpus, pruriens anima,* amorous conceits, tickling thoughts, sweet and pleasant thoughts; hence it is, they can think, discourse willingly, or speak almost of no other subject. 'Tis their only desire, if it may be done by art, to see their husband's picture in a glass, they'll give anything to know when they shall be married, how many husbands they shall have, by cromnyomantia, a kind of divination with onions laid on the altar on Christmas eve, or by fasting on St. John's eve or night, to know who shall be their first husband, or by amphitomantia, by means of a cake, &c., to burn the same. This love is the cause of all good conceits, neatness, exornations, plays, elegancies, delights, pleasant expressions, sweet notions, and gestures, joys, comforts, exultancies, and all the sweetness of our life, *qualis jam vita foret, aut quid jucundi sine aurea Venere? Emoriar cum istâ non amplius mihi cura fuerit,* let me live no longer than I may love, saith a mad merry fellow in Mimnermus. This love is that salt that seasoneth our harsh and dull labours, and gives a pleasant relish to our other unsavoury proceedings, *Absit amor, surgunt tenebræ, torpedo, veterum, pestis,* &c. All our feasts almost, masques, mummings, banquets, merry meetings, weddings, attelans, jigs, fescenines, elegies, odes, &c. proceed hence.... Apollo was the first inventor of physic, divination, oracles; Minerva found out weaving, Vulcan curious ironwork, Mercury letters, but who prompted all this into their heads? Love....

The Anatomy of Melancholy, Part 3. Sec. 2.

Anthony Wood

MUSIC IN OXFORD DURING THE COMMONWEALTH

BY THIS time A.W. had genuine skill in musick, and frequented the weekly meetings of musitians in the house of William Ellis, late organist of S. John's Coll., situat and being in a house opposite to that place whereon the Theatre was built. . . .

The musick masters, who were now in Oxon and frequented the said meeting, were (1) William Ellis, bach. of musick, owner of the house wherein the meeting was. He alwaies play'd his part either on the organ or virginal. (2) Dr. John Wilson, the public professor, the best at the lute in all England. He sometimes play'd on the lute, but mostly presided [1] the consort. (3) . . . Curteys a lutenist lately ejected from some choire or cath. church. After his majestie's restoration he became gent. or singing-man of Ch. Church in Oxon. (4) Thomas Jackson, a bass-violist; afterwards one of the choire of S. John's Coll. in Oxon. (5) Edward Low, organist lately of Ch. Church. He play'd only on the organ; so when he performed his part, Mr. Ellis would take up a counter-tenor viol and play, if any person were wanting to performe that part. (6) Gervace Littleton *alias* Westcot, or Westcot *alias* Littleton, a violist. He was afterwards a singing man of S. John's Coll. (7) William Flexney, who had belonged to a choire before the warr. He was afterwards a gent. or singing-man of Ch. Ch. He play'd well upon the bass-viol and sometimes sung his part. He died 6 Nov. 1692 aged 79 or thereabouts. (8) . . . Proctor a young man and a new commer. He died soon after as I shall tell you anon.—John Parker, one of the Universitie musitians, would be sometimes among them; but Mr. Low, a proud man, could not endure any common musitian to come to the meeting, much less to play among them. —Among these I must put John Haselwood an apothecary, a starched formal clisterpipe, who usually play'd on the bass-viol

[1] Directed.

and sometimes on the counter-tenor. He was very conceited of his skil (tho he had but little of it) and therefore would be ever and anon ready to take up a viol before his betters: which being observed by all, they usually called him *Handlewood*.

Thomas Balsar or Baltzar, a Lubecker borne, and the most famous artist for the violin that the world had yet produced, was now in Oxon; and this day A.W. was with him and Mr. Edward Low, lately organist of Ch. Church, at the meeting-house of William Ellis. A.W. did then and there, to his very great astonishment, heare him play on the violin. He then saw him run his fingers to the end of the finger-board of the violin, and run them back insensibly, and all with alacrity and in very good tune, which he nor any in England saw the like before. A.W. entertained him and Mr. Low with what the house could then afford, and afterwards he invited them to the tavern; but they being engag'd to goe to other company, he could no more heare him play nor see him play at that time. Afterwards he came to one of the weekly meetings at Mr. Ellis's house and he played to the wonder of all the auditory: and exercising his fingers and instrument several ways to the utmost of his power, Wilson thereupon, the public professor, (the greatest judge of musick that ever was) did, after his humoursome way, stoop down to Baltzar's feet, to see whether he had a huff on, that is to say to see whether he was a devill or not, because he acted beyond the parts of man.

About this time it was that Dr. John Wilkins, warden of Wadham Coll., the greatest curioso of his time, invited him and some of the musitians to his lodgings in that coll. purposely to have a consort and to see and heare him play. The instruments and books were carried thither, but none could be perswaded there to play against him in consort on the violin. At length the company perceiving A.W. standing behind, in a corner neare the dore, they haled him in among them, and play forsooth he must against him. Whereupon he being not able to avoid it, he took up a violin, and behaved himself as poor Troylus did against Achilles. He was abash'd at it, yet honour he got by playing with, and against, such a grand master as Baltzar was. Mr. Davis Mell was accounted hitherto the best for the violin in England, as I have before told you; but after Baltzar came into England and show'd his most wonderful parts on that instrument, Mell was not so admired; yet he play'd sweeter, and was a well bred gentleman and not given to excessive drinking as Baltzar was.

All the time that A.W. could spare from his beloved studies of English history, antiquities, heraldry and genalogies, he spent in the most delightful facultie of musick, either instrumental or vocal: and if he had missed the weekly meetings in the house of William Ellis, he could not well enjoy himself all the week after. All or most of the company, when he frequented that meeting, the names of them are set downe under the yeare 1656. . . .

These did frequent the weekly meetings; and by the help of publick masters of musick, who were mixed with them, they were much improv'd. Narcissus Marsh, M.A. and fellow of Exeter Coll., would come somtimes among them, but seldome play'd, because he had a weekly meeting in his chamber in the said Coll. where masters of musick would come and some of the company before mentioned. When he became principal of S. Alban's Hall, he translated the meeting thither, and there it continued when that meeting in Mr. Ellis's house was given over, and so it continued till he went to Ireland and became Mr. of Trinity Coll. at Dublin. He was afterwards archb. of Tuam in Ireland.

After his majestie's restoration, when then the masters of musick were restored to their several places that they before had lost, or else if they had lost none, they had gotten then preferment, the weekly meetings at Mr. Ellis's house began to decay, because they were held up only by scholars, who wanted directors and instructors, &c. so that in few yeares after, the meeting in that house being totally laid aside.

The Life and Times of Anthony Wood,
antiquary, of Oxford, 1632-1695, described
by Himself.

March, 1656; July, 1658; March-April 1659.

Thos. Fuller

WILLIAM LAWES

WILLIAM LAWES, son of Thomas Lawes, a vicar choral of the church of Salisbury, was bred in the Close of that city, being from his childhood inclined to music. Edward earl of Hertford obtained him from his father, and bred him at his own cost in that faculty, under his master Giovani Coperario,[1] an Italian, and most exquisite musician. Yet may it be said that the scholar in time did *equal*, yea *exceed*, his master.

He afterwards was of the private music to king Charles; and was respected and beloved of all such persons who cast any looks towards virtue and honour. Besides his fancies of the three, four, five, and six parts to viol and organ, he made above thirty several sorts of music for voices and instruments; neither was there any instrument then in use but he composed to it so aptly as if he had only studied that.

In these distracted times his loyalty engaged him in the war for his lord and master; and though he was by general Gerrard made a commissary, on design to secure him (such officers being commonly shot-free by their place, as not exposed to danger), yet such the activity of his spirit, he disclaimed the covert of his office, and betrayed thereunto by his own adventurousness, was casually shot at the siege of Chester, the same time when the lord Bernard Stuart lost his life.

Nor was the king's soul so engrossed with grief for the death of so near a kinsman, and noble lord, but that, hearing of the death of his dear servant William Lawes, he had a particular mourning for him when *dead*, whom he loved when *living*, and commonly called "the Father of Music". I leave the rest of his worth to be expressed by his own works of composures of Psalms done jointly by him and his brother, Master Henry Lawes, betwixt which two no difference, either in eminency, affection, or otherwise considerable, save that the one is deceased, and the

[1] John Cooper, born in England.

other still surviving. Master William Lawes died in September 1645.

The History of the Worthies of England, Vol. III.

John Milton

CHARACTER-BUILDING

THE COURSE of Study hitherto briefly described is, what I can guess by reading, likest to those ancient and famous Schools of *Pythagoras*, *Plato*, *Isocrates*, *Aristotle* and such others, out of which were bred up such a number of renowned philosophers, orators, historians, poets and princes all over *Greece*, *Italy* and *Asia*, besides the flourishing Studies of *Cyrene* and *Alexandria*. But herein it shall exceed them, and supply a defect as great as that which *Plato* noted in the common-wealth of *Sparta;* whereas that city trained up their youth most for war, and these in their *Academies* and *Lycæum*, all for the gown, this institution of breeding which I here delineate, shall be equally good both for peace and war. Therefore about an hour and a half ere they eat at noon should be allowed them for exercise and due rest afterwards: but the time for this may be enlarged at pleasure, according as their rising in the morning shall be early.

The exercise which I commend first is the exact use of their weapon, to guard and to strike safely with edge, or point; this will keep them healthy, nimble, strong, and well in breath, is also the likeliest means to make them grow large and tall, and to inspire them with a gallant and fearless courage, which being tempered with seasonable lectures and precepts to them of true fortitude and patience, will turn into a native and heroic valour, and make them hate the cowardice of doing wrong. They must be also practised in all the locks and grips of Wrestling, wherein English men were wont to excel, as need may often be in fight to tug or grapple, and to close. And this perhaps will be enough, wherein to prove and heat their single strength.

The interim of unsweating themselves regularly, and convenient rest before meat may both with profit and delight be taken up in recreating and composing their travailed spirits with the solemn and divine harmonies of Music heard or learnt; either while the skilful *Organist* plies his grave and fancied descant, in lofty fugues, or the whole symphony with artful and unimaginable touches adorn and grace the well studied chords of some choice composer, sometimes the lute, or soft organ stop waiting on elegant voices either to religious, martial, or civil Ditties; which, if wise men and Prophets be not extremely out, have a great power over dispositions and manners, to smoothe and make them gentle from rustic harshness and distempered passions. The like also would not be unexpedient after meat to assist and cherish Nature in her first concoction, and send their minds back to study in good tune and satisfaction. Where having followed it close under vigilant eyes till about two hours before supper, they are by a sudden alarum or watch word, to be called out to their military motions, under sky or covert, according to the season, as was the Roman wont.

Tractate of Education.

John Bunyan

THE CELESTIAL CITY

NOW YOU must note that the city stood upon a hill, but the pilgrims went up that hill with ease, because they had these two men to lead them up by the arms; also, they had left their mortal garments behind them in the river, for though they went in with them, they came out without them. They, therefore, went up here with much agility and speed, though the foundation upon which the city was framed was higher than the clouds. They, therefore, went up through the regions of the air, sweetly talking as they went, being comforted, because they safely got over the river, and had such glorious companions to attend them.

The talk they had with the Shining Ones was about the glory of the place; who told them that the beauty and glory of it was inexpressible. There, said they, is the "Mount Zion, the heavenly Jerusalem, the innumerable company of angels, and the spirits of just men made perfect" (Heb. xii. 22-24). You are going now, said they, to the paradise of God, wherein you shall see the tree of life, and eat of the never-fading fruits thereof; and when you come there, you shall have white robes given you, and your walk and talk shall be every day with the King, even all the days of eternity. (Rev. ii. 7; iii. 4; xxii. 5.) There you shall not see again such things as you saw when you were in the lower region upon the earth, to wit, sorrow, sickness, affliction, and death, "for the former things are passed away". You are now going to Abraham, to Isaac, and Jacob, and to the prophets—men that God hath taken away from the evil to come, and that are now resting upon their beds, each one walking in his righteousness. (Isa. lvii. 1,2; lxv. 17.) The men then asked, What must we do in the holy place? To whom it was answered, You must there receive the comforts of all your toil, and have joy for all your sorrow; you must reap what you have sown, even the fruit of all your prayers, and tears, and sufferings for the King by the way. (Gal. vi. 7.) In that place you must wear crowns of gold, and enjoy the perpetual sight and vision of the Holy One, for "there you shall see him as he is" (I John iii. 2.) There also you shall serve him continually with praise, with shouting, and thanksgiving, whom you desired to serve in the world, though with much difficulty, because of the infirmity of your flesh. There your eyes shall be delighted with seeing, and your ears with hearing the pleasant voice of the Mighty One. There you shall enjoy your friends again, that are gone thither before you; and there you shall with joy receive, even every one that follows into the holy place after you. There also shall you be clothed with glory and majesty, and put into an equipage fit to ride out with the King of glory. When he shall come with sound of trumpet in the clouds, as upon the wings of the wind, you shall come with him; and when he shall sit upon the throne of judgment, you shall sit by him;

yea, and when he shall pass sentence upon the workers of iniquity, let them be angels or men, you also shall have a voice in that judgment, because they were his and your enemies. (I Thess. iv. 13-17; Jude 14; Dan. vii. 9, 10; Cor. vi. 2,3.) Also, when he shall again return to the city, you shall go too, with sound of trumpet, and be ever with him.

Now while they were thus drawing towards the gate, behold a company of the heavenly host came out to meet them; to whom it was said, by the other two Shining Ones, These are the men that have loved our Lord when they were in the world, and that have left all for his holy name; and he hath sent us to fetch them, and we have brought them thus far on their desired journey, that they may go in and look their Redeemer in the face with joy. Then the heavenly host gave a great shout, saying, "Blessed are they which are called unto the marriage supper of the Lamb" (Rev. xix. 9). There came out also at this time to meet them, several of the King's trumpeters, clothed in white and shining raiment, who, with melodious noises, and loud, made even the heavens to echo with their sound. These trumpeters saluted Christian and his fellow with ten thousand welcomes from the world; and this they did with shouting, and sound of trumpet.

This done, they compassed them round on every side; some went before, some behind, and some on the right hand, some on the left (as it were to guard them through the upper regions), continually sounding as they went, with melodious noise, in notes on high: so that the very sight was to them that could behold it, as if heaven itself was come down to meet them. Thus, therefore, they walked on together; and as they walked, ever and anon these trumpeters, even with joyful sound, would, by mixing their music with looks and gestures, still signify to Christian and his brother, how welcome they were into their company, and with what gladness they came to meet them; and now were these two men, as it were, in heaven, before they came at it, being swallowed up with the sight of angels, and with hearing of their melodious notes. Here also they had the city itself in view, and they thought they heard all the bells within to ring, to welcome them thereto. But above all, the warm and joyful thoughts that they had about their own dwelling there, with such company, and that for ever and ever. Oh, by what tongue or pen can their glorious joy be expressed! And thus they came up to the gate.

Now, when they were come up to the gate, there was written over it in letters of gold, "Blessed are they that do his commandments, that they have right to the tree of life, and may enter in through the gates into the city." (Rev. xxii. 14.)

Then I saw in my dream, that the Shining Men bid them call at the gate; the which, when they did, some looked from above over the gate, to wit, Enoch, Moses, and Elijah &c., to whom it was said, These pilgrims are come from the City of Destruction, for the love that they bear to the King of this place; and then the pilgrims gave in unto them each man his certificate, which they had received in the beginning; those, therefore, were carried in to the King, who, when he had read them, said, Where are the men? To whom it was answered. They are standing without the gate. The King then commanded to open the gate, "That the righteous nation", said he, "which keepeth the truth, may enter in" (Isa. xxvi. 2).

Now I saw in my dream that these two men went in at the gate: and lo, as they entered, they were transfigured, and they had raiment put on that shone like gold. There were also that met them with harps and crowns, and gave them to them—the harps to praise withal, and the crowns in token of honour. Then I heard in my dream that all the bells in the city rang again for joy, and that it was said unto them, "ENTER YE INTO THE JOY OF YOUR LORD." I also heard the men themselves, that they sang with a loud voice, saying, "BLESSING AND HONOUR, AND GLORY, AND POWER, BE UNTO HIM THAT SITTETH UPON THE THRONE, AND UNTO THE LAMB, FOR EVER AND EVER" (Rev. v. 13).

Now, just as the gates were opened to let in the men, I looked in after them, and, behold, the City shone like the sun; the streets were paved with gold, and in them walked many men, with crowns on their heads, palms in their hands, and golden harps to sing praises withal.

There were also of them that had wings, and they answered one another without intermission, saying, "Holy, holy, holy is the Lord" (Rev. iv. 8). And after that they shut up the gates; which, when I had seen, I wished myself among them.

The Pilgrim's Progress from this world to that which is to come.

Samuel Pepys

OPINION

November 15th, 1667.

TO WESTMINSTER, and do hear that there is to be a conference between the two Houses to-day; so I stayed: and it was only to tell the Commons that the Lords cannot agree to the confining or sequestring of the Earl of Clarendon from the Parliament, forasmuch as they do not specify any particular crime which they lay upon him and call Treason. This the House did receive, and so parted: at which, I hear, the Commons are like to grow very high, and will insist upon their privileges, and the Lords will own theirs, though the Duke of Buckingham, Bristoll, and others, have been very high in the House of Lords to have had him committed. This is likely to breed ill blood. Home, and there find, as I expected, Mr. Caesar and little Pelham Humphreys, lately returned from France, and is an absolute Monsieur, as full of form, and confidence, and vanity, and disparages everything, and everybody's skill but his own. But to hear how he laughs at all the King's musick here, as Blagrave and others, that they cannot keep time nor tune, nor understand anything; and that Grebus, the Frenchman, the King's master of the musick, how he understands nothing, nor can play on any instrument, and so cannot compose: and that he will give him a lift out of his place; and that he and the King are mighty great! The King hath, as Mr. Moore says Sir Thomas Crewe told him, been heard to say that the quarrel is not between my Lord Chancellor and him, but his brother and him; which will make sad work among us if that be once promoted, as to be sure it will, Buckingham and Bristoll being now the only counsel the King follows, so as Arlington and Coventry are come to signify little. He tells me they are likely to fall upon my Lord Sandwich; but, for my part, sometimes I am apt to think they cannot do him much harm, he telling me that there is no great fear of the business of Resumption. This day, Poundy, the waterman, was with me, to let me know that he was summonsed to bear witness against me to Prince Rupert's people, who have a commission to look after the business of prize-goods, about the business of prize-goods I was concerned in: but I did desire him to speak all he knew, and not to spare me, nor did promise nor give him any thing, but sent him away with good words.

16th. To White Hall, where there is to be a performance of musick of Pelham's before the King. The company not come; but I did go into the musick-room, where Captain Cocke and many others; and here I did hear the best and the smallest organ go that ever I saw in my life, and such a one as, by the grace of God, I will have the next year, if I continue in this condition, whatever it cost me. Met Mr. Gregory, my old acquaintance, an understanding gentleman; and he and I walked an hour together, talking of the bad prospect of the times; and the sum of what I learn from him is this: That the King is the most concerned in the world against the Chancellor, and all people that do appear against him, and therefore is angry with the Bishops, having said that he had one Bishop on his side, Crofts, and but one: that Buckingham and Bristoll are now his only Cabinet Council; and that, before the Duke of York fell sick, Buckingham was admitted to the King of his Cabinet, and there stayed with him several hours, and the Duke of York, shut out. That it is plain that there is dislike between the King and Duke of York, and that it is to be feared that the House will go so far against the

Chancellor, that they must do something to undo the Duke of York, or will not think themselves safe. That this Lord Vaughan, that is so great against the Chancellor, is one of the lewdest fellows of the age, worse than Sir Charles Sedley; and that he was heard to swear he would do my Lord Clarendon's business. That he do find that my Lord Clarendon hath more friends in both Houses than he believes he would have, by reason that they do see what are the hands that pull him down; which they do not like. That Harry Coventry was scolded at by the King severly the other day; and that his answer was that, if he must not speak what he thought in this business in Parliament, he must not come thither. And he says that by this very business Harry Coventry hath got more fame and common esteem than any gentleman in England hath at this day, and is an excellent and able person. That the King, who not long ago did say of Bristoll, that he was a man able in three years to get himself a fortune in any kingdom in the world, and lose all again in three months, do now hug him, and commend his parts every where, above all the world. How fickle is this man [the King] and how unhappy we like to be! That he fears some furious courses will be taken against the Duke of York; and that he hath heard that it was designed, if they cannot carry matters against the Chancellor, to impeach the Duke of York himself; which God forbid! That Sir Edward Nicholas, whom he served while Secretary, is one of the best men in the world, but hated by the Queen-Mother, for a service he did the old King against her mind and her favourites; and that she and my Lady Castlemaine did make the King to lay him aside: but this man [Gregory] says that he is one of the most heavenly and charitable men in the whole world. That the House of Commons resolve to stand by their proceedings, and have chosen a Committee to draw up the reasons thereof to carry to the Lords; which is likely to breed great heat between them. That the Parliament, after all this, is likely to give the King no money; and, therefore, that it is to be wondered what makes the King give way to so great extravagancies, which do all tend to the making him less than he is, and so will, every day more and more: and by this means every creature is divided against the other, that there never was so great an uncertainty in England, of what would be the event of things, as at this day; nobody being at ease, or safe. To White Hall; and there got into the theatre-room, and there heard both the vocall and instrumentall musick; where the little fellow [Pelham Humfrey] stood keeping time; but for my part, I see no great matter, but quite the contrary in both sorts of musick. Here was the King and Queen, and some of the ladies; among whom none more jolly than my Lady Buckingham, her Lord being once more a great man.

Diary.

John Dryden

PREFACE TO "ALBION AND ALBANIUS"

IF WIT has truly been defined, "a propriety of thoughts and words", then that definition will extend to all sorts of poetry; and among the rest, to this present entertainment of an opera. Propriety of thought is that fancy which rises naturally from the subject, or which the poet adapts to it; propriety of words is the clothing of those thoughts with such expressions as are naturally proper to them; and from both these, if they are judiciously performed, the delight of poetry results. An opera is a poetical tale or fiction, represented by vocal and instrumental music, adorned with scenes, machines, and dancing. The supposed persons of this musical drama are generally supernatural, as gods, and goddesses, and heroes, which at least are descended from them, and are in due time to be adopted into their number. The subject, therefore, being extended beyond the limits of human nature, admits of that sort of marvellous and surprising conduct, which is rejected in other plays. Human impossibilities are to be received as they are in faith; because, where gods are introduced, a supreme power is to be understood, and second causes are out of doors; yet propriety is to be observed even here. The gods are all to manage their peculiar provinces; and what was attributed by the heathens to one power, ought not to be performed by any other. Phoebus must foretel, Mercury must charm with his caduceus, and Juno must reconcile the quarrels of the marriage-bed; to conclude, they must all act according to their distinct and peculiar characters. If the persons represented were to speak upon the stage, it would follow, of necessity, that the expressions should be lofty, figurative, and majestical; but the nature of an opera denies the frequent use of these poetical ornaments; for vocal music, though it often admits a loftiness of sound, yet always exacts an harmonious sweetness; or, to distinguish yet more justly, the recitative part of the opera requires a more masculine beauty of expression and sound. The other, which, for want of a proper English word, I must call the *songish part*, must abound in the softness and variety of numbers; its principal intention being to please the hearing, rather than to gratify the understanding. It appears, indeed, preposterous at first sight, that rhyme, on any consideration, should take place of reason; but, in order to resolve this problem, this fundamental proposition must be settled, that the first inventors of any art or science, provided they have brought it to perfection, are, in reason, to give laws to it; and, according to their model, all aftertakers are to build. Thus, in epic poetry, no man ought to dispute the authority of Homer, who gave the first being to that masterpiece of art, and endued it with that form of perfection in all its parts, that nothing was wanting to its excellency. Virgil, therefore, and those very few who have succeeded him, endeavoured not to introduce, or innovate any thing in a design already perfected, but imitated the plan of the inventor; and are only so far true heroic poets, as they have built on the foundations of Homer. Thus, Pindar, the author of those Odes, which are so admirably restored by Mr. Cowley in our language, ought for ever to be the standard of them; and we are bound, according to the practice of Horace and Mr. Cowley, to copy him. Now, to apply this axiom to our present purpose, whoever undertakes the writing of an opera, which is a modern invention, though built indeed on the foundation of ethnic worship, is obliged to imitate the design of the Italians, who have not only invented, but brought to perfection, this sort of dramatic musical entertainment. I have not been able, by any search, to get any light, either of the time when it began, or of the first author; but I have probable reasons, which induce me to believe, that some Italians, having curiously observed the gallantries of the Spanish Moors at their zambras, or royal feasts, where music, songs, and dancing, were in perfection, together with their machines, which are usual at their *sortijas*, or running at the ring, and other solemnities, may possibly have refined upon those Moresque divertisements, and produced this delightful entertainment, by leaving out the warlike part of the carousals, and forming a poetical design for the use of the machines, the songs, and dances. But however it began, (for this is only conjectural,) we know, that, for some centuries, the knowledge of music has flourished principally in Italy, the mother of learning and of arts; that poetry and painting have been there restored, and so cultivated by Italian masters, that all Europe has been enriched out of their treasury; and the other parts of it, in relation to those delightful arts, are still as much provincial to Italy, as they were in the time of the Roman empire. Their first operas seem to have been intended for the celebrations of the marriages of their princes, or for the magnificence of some general time of joy; accordingly, the expenses of them were from the purse of the sovereign, or of the republic, as they are still practised at Venice, Rome, and at other places, at their carnivals. Savoy and Florence have often used them in their courts, at the weddings of their dukes; and at Turin particularly, was performed the "Pastor Fido", written by the famous Guarini, which is a pastoral opera made to solemnise the marriage of a Duke of Savoy. The prologue of it has given the design to all the French; which is a compliment to the sovereign power by some god or goddess; so that it looks no less than a kind of embassy from heaven to earth. I said in the beginning of this preface, that the persons represented in operas are generally gods,

goddesses, and heroes descended from them, who are supposed
to be their peculiar care; which hinders not, but that meaner
persons may sometimes gracefully be introduced, especially
if they have relations to those first times, which poets call the
Golden Age; wherein, by reason of their innocence, those happy
mortals were supposed to have had a more familiar intercourse
with superior beings; and therefore shepherds might reasonably
be admitted, as of all callings the most innocent, the most happy,
and who, by reason of the spare time they had, in their most idle
employment, had most leisure to make verses, and to be in
love; without somewhat of which passion, no opera can possibly
subsist.

It is almost needless to speak any thing of that noble language,
in which this musical drama was first invented and performed.
All, who are conversant in the Italian, cannot but observe, that
it is the softest, the sweetest, the most harmonious, not only of
any modern tongue, but even beyond any of the learned. It
seems indeed to have been invented for the sake of poetry and
music; the vowels are so abounding in all words, especially in
terminations of them, that, excepting some few monosyllables,
the whole language ends in them. Then the pronunciation is so
manly, and so sonorous, that their very speaking has more of
music in it than Dutch poetry and song. It has withall derived
so much copiousness and elegance from the Greek and Latin,
in the composition of words, and the formation of them, that
if, after all, we must call it barbarous, it is the most beautiful
and most learned of any barbarism in modern tongues; and we
may, at least, as justly praise it, as Pyrrhus did the Roman
discipline and martial order, that it was of barbarians, (for so
the Greeks called all other nations,) but had nothing in it of
barbarity. This language has in a manner been refined and
purified from the Gothic ever since the time of Dante,· which
is above four hundred years ago; and the French, who now cast
a longing eye to their country, are not less ambitious to possess
their elegance in poetry and music; in both which they labour
at impossibilities. It is true, indeed, they have reformed their

tongue, and brought both their prose and poetry to a standard; the sweetness, as well as the purity, is much improved, by throwing off the unnecessary consonants, which made their spelling tedious, and their pronunciation harsh; but, after all, as nothing can be improved beyond its own *species*, or farther than its original nature will allow; as an ill voice, though ever so thoroughly instructed in the rules of music, can never be brought to sing harmoniously, nor many an honest critic ever arrive to be a good poet; so neither can the natural harshness of the French, or their perpetual ill accent, be ever refined into perfect harmony like the Italian. The English has yet more natural disadvantages than the French; our original Teutonic, consisting most in monosyllables, and those incumbered with consonants, cannot possibly be freed from those inconveniences. The rest of our words, which are derived from the Latin chiefly, and the French, with some small sprinklings of Greek, Italian, and Spanish, are some relief in poetry, and help us to soften our uncouth numbers; which, together with our English genius, incomparably beyond the trifling of the French, in all the nobler parts of verse, will justly give us the pre-eminence. But, on the other hand, the effeminacy of our pronunciation, (a defect common to us and the Danes,) and our scarcity of female rhimes, have left the advantage of musical composition for songs, though not for recitative, to our neighbours.

Through these difficulties I have made a shift to struggle in my part of the performance of this opera; which, as mean as it is, deserves at least a pardon, because it has attempted a discovery beyond any former undertaken of our nation; only remember, that if there be no north-west passage to be found, the fault is in nature, and not in me; or, as Ben Jonson tells us in "The Alchymist", when projection had failed, and the glasses were all broken, there was enough, however, in the bottoms of them, to cure the itch; so I may thus be positive, that if I have not succeeded as I desire, yet there is somewhat still remaining to satisfy the curiosity, or itch of sight and hearing. Yet I have no great reason to despair; for I may, without vanity, own some advantages, which are not common to every writer; such as are the knowledge of the Italian and French language, and the being conversant with some of their best performances of this kind; which have furnished me with such variety of measures, as have given the composer, Monsieur Grabut, what occasions he could wish, to shew his extraordinary talent in diversifying the recitative, the lyrical part, and the chorus; in all which, not to attribute any thing to my own opinion, the best judges, and those too of the best quality, who have honoured his rehearsals with their presence, have no less recommended the happiness of his genius than his skill. And let me have the liberty to add one thing, that he has so exactly expressed my sense in all places where I intended to move the passions, that he seems to have entered into my thoughts, and to have been the poet as well as the composer. This I say, not to flatter him, but to do him right; because amongst some English musicians, and their scholars, who are sure to judge after them, the imputation of being a Frenchman is enough to make a party, who maliciously endeavour to decry him. But the knowledge of Latin and Italian poets, both which he possesses, besides his skill in music, and his being acquainted with all the performances of the French operas, adding to these the good sense to which he is born, have raised him to a degree above any man, who shall pretend to be his rival on our stage. When any of our country-men excel him, I shall be glad, for the sake of Old England, to be shewn my error; in the mean time, let virtue be commended, though in the person of a stranger.

If I thought it convenient, I could here discover some rules which I have given to myself in writing of an opera in general, and of this opera in particular; but I consider, that the effect would only be, to have my own performance measured by the laws I gave; and, consequently, to set up some little judges, who, not understanding thoroughly, would be sure to fall upon the faults, and not to acknowledge any of the beauties; an hard measure, which I have often found from false critics. Here, therefore, if they will criticise, they shall do it out of their own *fond*; but let them first be assured that their ears are nice; for there is neither writing nor judgment on this subject without that good quality. It is no easy matter, in our language, to make words so smooth, and numbers so harmonious, that they shall almost set themselves. And yet there are rules for this in nature, and as great a certainty of quantity in our syllables, as either in the Greek or Latin: but let poets and judges understand those first, and then let them begin to study English. When they have chewed a while upon these preliminaries, it may be they will scarce adventure to tax me with want of thought and elevation of fancy in this work; for they will soon be satisfied, that those are not of the nature of this sort of writing. The necessity of double rhimes, and ordering of the words and numbers for the sweetness of the voice, are the main hinges on which an opera must move; and both of these are without the compass of any art to teach another to perform, unless nature, in the first place, has done her part, by enduing the poet with that nicety of hearing, that the discord of sounds in words shall as much offend him, as a seventh in music would a good composer. I have therefore no need to make excuses for meanness of thought in many places: the Italians, with all the advantages of their language, are continually forced upon it, or, rather, affect it. The chief secret is the choice of words; and, by this choice, I do not here mean elegancy of expression, but propriety of sound, to be varied according to the nature of the subject. Perhaps a time may come when I may treat of this more largely, out of some observations which I have made from Homer and Virgil, who, amongst all the poets, only understood the art of numbers, and of that which was properly called *rhythmus* by the ancients.

The same reasons, which depress thought in an opera, have a stronger effect upon the words, especially in our language; for there is no maintaining the purity of English in short measures, where the rhime returns so quick, and is so often female, or double rhime, which is not natural to our tongue, because it consists too much of monosyllables, and those, too, most commonly clogged with consonants; for which reason I am often forced to coin new words, revive some that are antiquated, and botch others;[1] as if I had not served out my time in poetry, but was bound apprentice to some doggrel rhimer, who makes songs to tunes, and sings them for a livelihood. It is true, I have not been found often put to this drudgery; but where I have, the words will sufficiently shew, that I was then a slave to the composition, which I will never be again: it is my part to invent, and the musician's to humour that invention. I may be counselled, and will always follow my friend's advice where I find it reasonable, but will never part with the power of the militia.

I am now to acquaint my reader with somewhat more particular concerning this opera, after having begged his pardon for so long a preface to so short a work. It was originally intended only for a prologue to a play of the nature of "The Tempest"; which is a tragedy mixed with opera, or a drama, written in blank verse, adorned with scenes, machines, songs, and dances, so that the fable of it is all spoken and acted by the best of the comedians; the other part of the entertainment to be performed by the same singers and dancers who were introduced in this present opera. It cannot properly be called a play, because the action of it is supposed to be conducted sometimes by supernatural means, or magic; nor an opera, because the story of it is not sung.—But more of this at its proper time.—But some intervening accidents having hitherto deferred the performance of the main design, I proposed to the actors, to turn the intended Prologue into an entertainment by itself, as you now see it, by adding two acts more to what I had already written. The subject of it is wholly allegorical; and the allegory itself so obvious, that it will no sooner be read than understood. It is divided, according to the plain and natural method of every action, into three parts. For even Aristotle himself is contented to say simply, that in all actions there is a beginning, a middle, and an end; after which model all the Spanish plays are built.

The descriptions of the scenes, and other decorations of the stage, I had from Mr. Betterton, who has spared neither for

---

[1] Dryden here disregards the possibilities of English consonants and monosyllables in music, which we know to be one of the glories of Henry Purcell's art.

industry, nor cost, to make the entertainment perfect, nor for invention of the ornaments to beautify it.

To conclude, though the enemies of the composer are not few, and that there is a party formed against him of his own profession, I hope, and am persuaded, that this prejudice will turn in the end to his advantage. For the greatest part of an audience is always uninterested, though seldom knowing; and if the music be well composed, and well performed, they, who find themselves pleased, will be so wise as not to be imposed upon, and fooled out of their satisfaction. The newness of the undertaking is all the hazard. When operas were first set up in France, they were not followed over eagerly; but they gained daily upon their hearers, till they grew to that height of reputation, which they now enjoy. The English, I confess, are not altogether so musical as the French; and yet they have been pleased already with "The Tempest", and some pieces that followed, which were neither much better written nor so well composed as this. If it finds encouragement, I dare promise myself to mend my hand, by making a more pleasing fable. In the mean time, every loyal Englishman cannot but be satisfied with the moral of this, which so plainly represents the double restoration of his Sacred Majesty.

POSTSCRIPT

This preface being wholly written before the death of my late royal master, (*quem semper acerbum semper honoratum, sic dii voluistis, habebo,*) I have now lately reviewed it, as supposing I should find many notions in it, that would require correction on cooler thoughts. After four months lying by me, I looked on it as no longer mine, because I had wholly forgotten it; but I confess with some satisfaction, and perhaps a little vanity, that I found myself entertained by it; my own judgment was new to me, and pleased me when I looked on it as another man's. I see no opinion that I would retract or alter, unless it be, that possibly the Italians went not so far as Spain, for the invention of their operas. They might have it in their own country; and that by gathering up the shipwrecks of the Athenian and Roman theatres, which we know were adorned with scenes, music, dances, and machines, especially the Grecian. But of this the learned Monsieur Vossius, who has made our nation his second country, is the best, and perhaps the only judge now living. As for the opera itself, it was all composed, and was just ready to have been performed, when he, in honour of whom it was principally made, was taken from us.

He had been pleased twice or thrice to command, that it should be practised before him, especially the first and third acts of it; and publicly declared, more than once, that the composition and choruses were more just, and more beautiful, than any he had heard in England. How nice an ear he had in music, is sufficiently known; his praise therefore has established the reputation of it above censure, and made it in a manner sacred. It is therefore humbly and religiously dedicated to his memory.

It might reasonably have been expected, that his death must have changed the whole fabric of the opera, or at least a great part of it. But the design of it was originally so happy, that it needed no alteration, properly so called; for the addition of twenty or thirty lines in the apotheosis of Albion, has made it entirely of a piece. This was the only way which could have been invented, to save it from botched ending; and it fell luckily into my imagination; as if there were a kind of fatality even in the most trivial things concerning the succession. A change was made, and not for the worse, without the least confusion or disturbance; and those very causes, which seemed to threaten us with troubles, conspired to produce our lasting happiness.

Book II

THE
AGE OF
REASON

HANDEL · DEFOE   NORTH · BOSWELL

B.G.S.

THE AGE OF REASON

THE HON. ROGER NORTH'S *Memoires of Musick* should not be overlooked in any effort to sum up the musical taste of England in the late seventeenth and early eighteenth centuries. His book is a personal document—he writes down what he himself has observed—but his training as a lawyer enabled him to concentrate on essentials. Whereas in the early part of the seventeenth century Henry Peacham had retailed all manner of tales about the music of the ancients, Roger North sifts the available information, provisionally accepting some and discarding some: giving reasons for the rejection. His legal training had something to do with this, but perhaps not everything, for he lived in an age when scientific inquiry had come to influence educated men.

It should be remembered that this was the age that saw the beginning of the Royal Society, which, though devoted to experimental science, "to increase the powers of all mankind and to free them from the bondage of errors", was open to all thinking men, and indeed owed a great deal to devotees of the arts. Both John Evelyn and John Dryden were prominent members, and Newton's *Principia* was issued in 1686 under the *imprimatur* of Samuel Pepys, as president. Science, religion and letters were complementary; out from their union in a more permanent way grew the new culture of the eighteenth century. They liked to think of it as an Augustan age, or an Age of Reason. It was a century rich in English prose, grand in painting and architecture, prosperous in worldly affairs.

Music changed, too: those were the days of the new concerts, innumerable clever musicians, and exceptional vocal ability.

"The Nation (as I may term it) of Musick was well prepared

for a revolution", wrote Roger North. "A great means of bringing that foreward was the humour of following publick consorts, and it will not be out of the way to deduce them from the beginning. The first of those was in a lane behind Paul's, where there was a chamber organ that one, Phillips, played upon, and some shopkeepers and foremen came weekly to sing in consort, and to hear and enjoy ale and tobacco; and after some time the audience grew strong." He describes also the public consort (the name has changed with the years to "concert") started by John Banister (one of Charles the Second's violinists) at Whitefriars, and a gentlemen's meeting, "whom I shall not name, for some of them as I hear are still living, that used to meet often for consort after Baptist's manner, and falling into a weekly course, and performing exceeding well with Bass violins[1] (a cours instrument as it was then, which they used to hire) their friends and acquaintance were admitted, and by degrees, as the fame of their meeting spread, so many auditors came that their room was crowded; and to prevent that inconvenience, they took a room in a Taverne in Fleet Street, and the taverner pretended to make formall seats, and to take money, and then the society disbanded."

Here we see the working-out of the opinion voiced by Henry Peacham. Playing for one's own satisfaction, either solo or in consort, was a suitable accomplishment for a gentleman; but how about those who wanted only to listen? They were certainly not regarded as badly brought up—whatever Morley may have said. They were treated with courtesy, as guests. The action of the landlord of the tavern where they met tainted this courtesy, made the relationship between the performers and the audience mercenary, and the old spirit could not be preserved.

This, however, was a gentleman's point of view. Among those who made their living in trade like the foremen and shop-keepers who met near to St. Paul's, such a point of view would be incongruous: the members of the audience paid for their own drinks.

[1] The Violoncello.

In the case of John Banister's public meetings there was no doubt on the issue, for Banister had to make a living by his art: "The room was rounded with seats and small tables, alehous fashion. One shilling was the price, and call for what you pleased." Banister's music was good, and there can be little justification for the view expressed by eighteenth century German critics, that because the English took money for their music, the art declined. In fact audiences who paid to hear music wanted their money's worth, and their taste became a factor in supply and demand. There is no one public for music, since that would imply a uniform standard of taste; concerts made different appeals— some tended towards high artistic standards, others towards standards easiest to supply; but whichever sort the individual member of the audience preferred, he tended to support the music best of its type. The greatest influence on musical taste during the eighteenth century was undoubtedly Italian opera. So highly developed was the technique of the Italian singers who came to this country, that opinion was sharply divided, some, like Addison, detesting the absurdities of this exotic art,[1] and others, like Dr. Burney, acknowledging the superior standards of performance these singers exhibited. Between these two considered opinions lay a mass of undeveloped opinion, mainly among those whose primary wish was to be in the fashion. They went to the opera to be seen, and the men ostentatiously hummed operatic airs in the coffee-houses ("the humming beaux", they were called) just to let everybody know that they had been there. From this habit Steele worked up a fine satire in the *Spectator*, adding to it a craze for dancing, and all the other vices of the enthusiastic bore. This was in 1711, when Handel had only just established himself among us, and—in spite of Addison's satire in the same journal—really was showing London something new in entertainment.

This was the age of great satire, leading to great caricature: *The Beggar's Opera* was to come, and Hogarth's cartoons. Nor were the known *literati* the only ones to join in the fun, for the

[1] Addison had failed to make his mark with it.

93

ballad-mongers continually had their say:

> O England! foreign fashion's easy dupe!
> To what hath love of pleasure made thee stoop?
> To the vile trash of Italy and France.
> One squeals, and t'other's cap'ring we call dance.[1]

The fashion for Italian singers spread to private houses, giving Dr. Charles Burney an opportunity for one of his choicest bits of prose:

> "As to such elegant *private concerts* as are now frequently given by the nobility and gentry at their own houses, they were at this time scarcely known. The first I remember were at Lady Brown's, under the direction of Count St. Germain. Her ladyship distinguished herself as a persevering enemy to Handel, and a protectress of foreign musicians in general, of the new Italian style; and was one of the first persons of fashion who had the courage, at the risk of her windows, to have concerts of a Sunday evening.
>
> The next remarkable *Academia*, that I remember to have occasioned much curiosity and speculation, was established in the house of Mrs. Fox Lane, afterwards Lady Bingley, on the arrival of Giardini in England. The superior talents of that performer were always warmly patronised by this lady to the time of her death; and not content with admiring him herself, she contrived every means that could be devised to make him the admiration of others. As Giardini was seldom to be heard in public after his first arrival, she invited very select parties of the first people in the kingdom to hear him at her house, for which happiness she did not suffer them to remain ungrateful at his benefit.
>
> When Mingotti arrived in this kingdom, having united her interests with those of Giardini in the conduct and management of the opera, Mrs. Lane espoused *her* cause with great

[1] Ballad of 1745.

zeal; entering into the spirit of all her theatrical quarrels as ardently as if they had been her own. With two such performers, the concerts she gave to her choice friends were subjects of envy and obliquy to all those who were unable to obtain admission. At these concerts Mrs. Lane frequently played the harpsichord herself; as did Lady Edgcumbe and the late Lady Milbanke, both admirable performers on that instrument. Lady Rockingham, the Dowager Lady Carlisle, and Miss Pelham, scholars of Giardini, and Mingotti, used to sing: and the difficulty, or rather impossibility, of hearing these professors and illustrious dilettanti any where else, stimulated curiosity so much, that there was no sacrifice or mortification to which fashionable people would not submit, in order to obtain admission. And *la padrona della casa* lost few opportunities of letting them know the value she set on her invitations, by using them like dogs when they were there. Whenever a benefit was in contemplation for one of her protégés, taking care of the honour of her guests, she obliged them to behave with due gratitude and munificence on the occasion: "Come!" would she often say to her friends, "give me five guineas",—a demand as implicitly obeyed as if made on the road. Nor had any one, who ever wished to be admitted to such good company again, the courage to ask the occasion of the demand; but patiently waited the lady's pleasure to tell them whether they should be honoured with a ticket for Giardini's or Mingotti's benefit."

There is ample evidence of the mixture of good and bad manners with the musical taste of the eighteenth century, nor did it all come from the social climbers; political feeling might be a cause, as in the case of Dr. Hearne's strictures on Handel and his players at Oxford, for Hearne was a Jacobite of a downright character. A wave of anti-Catholic opinion would cause oranges and eggs to be thrown in the Italian opera-house in the Haymarket. The Age of Reason was in many ways a sham. Yet the respect for reason often made for fairer judgment than the previous century had allowed. Burney stood for high artistic standards, according to the opinion of his day, and these brought him up against evils that debased the art he loved. There are some things the British have always held in abhorrence, and among these is the practice of castration.[1] The glory of the Italian opera was the adult male soprano; on him more than any other factor the vocal style of that art depended, and Burney, in defending his love of this music, has to accept a practice he cannot defend on humane grounds. Nevertheless Burney's defence of the *evirati* is a well-reasoned piece of writing. He will not allow these unfortunates to be convicted of cowardice or of weak mentality. Cowardly *castrati* there may have been, but all should not be condemned for a few. Burney's musical taste leads him into prejudice, however, when he quotes Della Valle's account of the ability of the *evirati* in the Sistine Chapel in the seventeenth century. This was really dangerous ground for an English writer to tread. The English church had never accepted the necessity for a true soprano[2] male voice, since the older practice of training church singers to use their falsetto register gave good results—and indeed still does in our cathedrals. Alto voices have a quality of their own, which English church composers used effectively in England during the time that music in Rome had changed under the influence of the *castrati*. Henry Purcell's natural voice was baritone, but he sang alto as well, using his trained falsetto range for the latter. This we can tell from the music he is known to have sung. Burney may quote an Italian on the superiority of adult male soprani over boys and adult male singers who used their falsetto register, and from his point of view he may be right, but in doing so Burney would come against a body of opinion that would see him hanged before it would admit that anything could justify castration. This body of opinion was not all given up solely to humanitarian convictions, but could point to our excellent school of English church music as an example of good taste in choral art. Handel had to take this into consideration when he held the post of director of music

---

[1] It was practised in England as one of the sadistic indignities imposed at the scaffold on the worst type of criminal.
[2] Boys' voices should properly be called treble.

to the Duke of Chandos. The grandiose Baroque style of the architecture of Canons reflects the Duke's taste—imitation Italian —but his chapel services were of the English church, and here Handel built up a choral style that blended traditional English style with a demand for worldly veneration. The trumpets resounded in the ornate ceiling, the voices opened out in bold harmonies, and all was glorious, if at times somewhat theatrical. Pope saw the shallowness of it all:

> And now the chapel's silver bell we hear,
> That summons us to all the pride of prayer;
> Light quips of music, broken and uneven,
> Make the soul dance upon a jig to heaven.

Handel, however, showed himself able to think in the English style as well as he did in the Italian style; while there he produced the first versions of *Esther* and *Acis and Galatea* that were to stand him in good stead later, when economic reasons not without relation to English taste were to direct his thoughts to oratorio.

The experience of Canons can hardly have been sufficient to turn Handel's attention to large-scale sacred music after he had left the Duke's service, however. Credit must be given to the popularity of his *Te Deum and Jubilate* (1713) for the Peace of Utrecht, and after 1743 the *Dettingen Te Deum*, both of which in praising God glorified a victorious nation. The nation liked this as much as did Queen Anne or George II. The best opportunities for the performance of such works came at the great charity festivals in our cathedrals, of which that of the Three Choirs—Worcester, Hereford and Gloucester—is the most important. The sermon preached by Dr. Thomas Bisse at one of these festivals, *Music: the Delight of the Sons of Men* epitomises the thought of that age, bending all to music and charity. Here we find not only the age-old theory of music as a balm to souls in travail, and a worthy means of praising God, but we are reminded of its importance in every aspect of life, in places of entertainment and in the Court. Bisse speaks of the influence of environment on the type of music required; court or sanctuary, theatre or home; and he tells how styles of music must be used for their appropriate task. This is true criticism: the application of scientific method to judgment of the art. Behind Bisse we can almost see the shadows of Berkley and of Newton, especially when he outlines the scientific basis of music in acoustics, and sees in this the perfect manifestation of the will of God. No more are we asked to marvel with Henry Peacham at the sympathy between two lutes tuned in unison, or why two brass pots "shall, stricken, be a just *Diapason* in sound one to the other"; to Dr. Bisse these are no mystery, but they are nevertheless ordained by God for His purpose. "Oh! that men would therefore praise him for his goodness upon this suitable occasion, and declare the wonders, which in the institution of harmony, and the formation of the objects and instruments in subservience to its enjoyment, I say, declare aloud the wonders that he doth for the children of men!" Here speaks the age of reason with the voice of impassioned prose.

Yet we shall miss the point of the Three Choirs Festivals unless we appreciate that their object was charity. There was great diversity of means within the Church of England. Some clergymen were very rich, many were pluralists, but others were too poor to educate their sons. The Three Choirs Festival provides a fund for this purpose, and in the eighteenth century this fund could also be used to help educate the sons of church musicians. The humbler clergy may not all have had the merits of Goldsmith's Vicar of Wakefield but theirs was a special problem nevertheless—they served by example and advice, and the quality of their tastes influenced those around them. Chapter 17 of *The Vicar of Wakefield* may be taken for an example of how music was enjoyed in a home that sought some refinement in a time of adversity. The pretty tunes sung at the London pleasure gardens served here their turn, and the lute of the previous century had now made way for the guitar. This was the so-called English guitar, however; (actually an Italian cittern that remained popular in England after the Spanish guitar had captured the Italian ear). The instrument had wire strings and a body almost round. The Vauxhall and Ranelagh songs stood in a third tradition—distinct from the style of the English church and far removed from the highly specialised songs of the Italian opera. Here were also happy tunes in the English ballad tradition—a tradition that served all men and all tastes with its great variety. If *The Beggar's Opera* in 1728 was a scathing social satire, it was also a successful pot-boiler, and the reason lay in the natural grace of the tunes. This grace the foreigner cannot capture—Dr. Pepusch wrote basses to the tunes of *The Beggar's Opera*, not the tunes themselves—and in truth it must be admitted that the foreigners had little use for English ballad style, since the public took well enough to foreign styles when they were of the right quality. Boyce could command the English melodic muse well enough on occasion, and wrote graceful music for the Three Choirs Festivals, some of which he hoped might prove popular in the London Pleasure Gardens. His overtures, and especially the Symphony in D minor known as the *Worcester Symphony* might well be heard more frequently; they compare favourably with the music of other composers working in London at that time.

The Age of Reason saw some strange criticism of music, but reason rarely won the day. Even the oracular Samuel Johnson had a good ear, though he would have denied it. His melodic sense was weak, if Boswell's account of his evening's entertainment at Ashbourne is to be taken at its face value, yet he used rhythm in prose with a natural facility. "To *make* money is to *coin* it: you should say *get* money." The essential words are placed on the accent, and are sharply distinct from each other in sound. The ear decides the choice of word and its place in the sentence. Yet Johnson might have avowed robustly that he was concerned only with the factor of common-sense in prose; and how right he would have been! Such facility is the result of intellect allied to a feeling of aptness, and the root of the word "sense" meant feeling. It was not feeling that Johnson really objected to, but uncontrolled emotion, when Boswell told him that music affected him to such a degree as often to agitate his nerves painfully, producing in his mind alternate sensations of pathetic dejection and daring resolution. "Sir", said Samuel, "I should never hear it, if it made me such a fool."

Yet Boswell was no fool. He had this experience, and he tried to understand it. He realised as few men did that his emotional reactions to music were influenced by associations. Such things happen to men, and affect their taste; it is not given to everyone to see the implications as clearly as Boswell did. A reasonable explanation of personal emotions is a most difficult thought to bring to fruition. It may even be impossible.

In this sort of thing the great prose writers of the eighteenth century are much more satisfactory than the musicians. Perhaps it is unfair to make a comparison between the two, if that comparison is not to be founded on the composer's true medium, which is music. Nevertheless we cannot help noticing the prevailing tendency for musicians to denounce their contemporaries unwisely, and to contradict themselves in statements about their art. When Sir John Hawkins wrote his *Memoir of Dr. Boyce* for the second edition of the *Cathedral Music* he would have done better to have used more judgment in sifting Boyce's opinions. Did John Christian Bach and Abel spoil English taste with tediously monotonous basses and such harmony as the ear sickens at hearing? Surely the explanation is that Bach and Abel were performers intent on presenting novelties to their concert audiences, whereas Boyce hoped that his compositions would attain permanent popularity like the Minuet from Handel's *Rodelinda*. In this he was disappointed, and it cannot be said that he was indifferent to applause and commendation. One suspects that Boyce sulked. He had the gift of melody, but he could be very tedious at times. Boyce's *Solomon*, a long Serenata composed for the Three Choirs Festival of 1743, was revived and performed in its entirety at Oxford in 1948. Despite many graceful parts the work palled, owing to long intermediate stretches of slight interest. Audiences chattered much in the eighteenth century, and there are times when one feels the musicians even expected it. As for Dibdin, at the end of the century, he was a great liar, but at times an entertaining one: it is pleasant to read how Dr. Elliston, Vice-Chancellor of Cambridge University, caught him out.

"Sir, I am going to India, and as I wish, before my departure, to bid adieu to a generous public, who have afforded me a long and liberal patronage—"
"Why, do you know any body at Cambridge?"
"No, Sir."

Both Boyce and Dibdin expected unqualified admiration for their art, when at times some attention to the opinions of others might have served them in good stead. This is not to say that outside opinion can decide the final state of a musical composition, for this can be decided by the mind of its creator alone, but it can show the line of criticism that may be encountered, and enable the composer to consider the justice of this in respect to his particular idea. There is a certain element of self-pity in the mentality of minor composers that often gives a clue to their failure. As with Dibdin:

"The world, as a social system, I never could comprehend. It always exhibited to my view a monstrous and unfathomable gulph, filled with heterogeneous materials, in which the various passions and desires are hurled about at random: restless, errant, and disjointed. Where everything is pursued, nothing attained; and where men seek fame and find only disappointment."

This is not true. Dibdin could always have satisfied himself with his songs, even though they failed to secure general approval. His tragedy was that so many of his songs were written for popular consumption, and when they failed to relish, Dibdin had no personal satisfaction from them. When the battle of Cape St. Vincent had aroused a patriotic fervour, Dibdin seized on it as a good subject for a song—which it was—but what did he produce?

> As for that noble victory
> That this battle well was fighted,
> All people, high and low degree,
> Are equally united.

> 'Tis in the mouths of all one meets,
> All praise this noble service;
> And ballad-singers in the streets
> Roar "Admirable Jervis".

Dibdin must have known he could do better, so where was his satisfaction? Though we may admit that in the moment of victory a sailor's grumble may be unpopular with landlubbers, we can appreciate today the sincerity of a true sailor's ballad of this period:

> "Damn and blast old Admiral Jervis,
> For he is no sailor's friend."

and appreciate that these men did not seek fame in their song, but something that always stirs humanity—justice. There have always been minds that in disappointment have revealed themselves great—in music as in everything else. Not all have turned to sentimentality. In the eighteenth century there were composers in London who suffered from comparison with Handel: of these Bononcini is the most quoted, but there was also Dr. Pepusch, whose early compositions were good, but the response unsatisfactory. Pepusch became soured but not sentimental. He married Margarita de l'Epine, a singer and harpsichord player of great fame, who had a fortune of £10,000, and an interest in old music which was shared by Pepusch himself. This interest in the music of former times was not common among composers of the eighteenth century, who liked to be up-to-date; it was, however, consistent with the new conception of scientific inquiry which the Royal Society fostered. Pepusch found his niche in the scheme, though in doing so he ran the risk of being misunderstood by the modernists. Thus Burney:

"The sole ambition of Pepusch, during the last years of his life, seems to have been the obtaining the reputation of a profound theorist, perfectly skilled in the Music of the ancients; and attaching himself to the mathematician De Moivre and Geo. Lewis Scot, who helped him to calculate ratios and construe the Greek writers on Music, he bewildered himself and some of his scholars with the Greek genera, scales, diagrams, geometrical, arithmetical, and harmonical proportions, surd quantities, apotomes, lemmas, and every thing concerning ancient harmonies, that was dark, unintelligible, and foreign to common and useful practice. But with all his pedantry and ideal admiration for the Music of the ancients, he certainly had read more books on the theory of modern Music, and examined more curious compositions, than any of the musicians of his time; and though totally devoid of fancy and invention, he was able to correct the productions of his contempories, and to assign reasons for whatever he had done by the greatest masters who preceded him. But when he was called the most learned of his time it should be said, in the Music of the sixteenth century. Indeed, he had at last such a partiality for musical mysteries, and a spirit so truly antiquarian, that he allowed no composition to be Music but what was old and obscure. Yet, though he fettered the genius of his scholars with antiquated rules, he knew the mechanical laws of harmony so well, that in glancing his eye over a score, he could by a stroke of his pen, smooth the wildest and most incoherent notes into melody, and make them submissive to harmony; instantly seeing the superfluous or deficient notes and suggesting a base from which there was no appeal."

With Pepusch the new spirit of scientific inquiry mixed with

art to make musicology. Dr. Pepusch saved for us the Fitzwilliam
Virginal Book, and that alone is enough to counteract any
charge Burney made against him. In any case some of the music
of Pepusch is available, and it is not "totally devoid of fancy
and invention" by any means. Scientific inquiry led to remarkable progress in all phases of life during the eighteenth century;
no longer could men let their fancies rove unbounded; now
there was a closer adherence to known facts. Yet though the
essence of scientific research was in the exchange of ideas, and
making freely known to all interested men the latest theory or
discovery, this was done with a greater respect for individual
effort and enterprise than ever before. It was every man's duty
to seek his own advancement, according to the belief of the time,
and the advancement of the nation as a whole depended on the
private acquisitions of each citizen. Agriculture was improved,
and wealth came with this improvement to the enterprising
landowner: mechanical power started to transform industry
and the grouping of population. With wealth came a desire
for elegance, and better opportunities for social advancement.
London architecture tells the story as part of a continued history,
but the city of Bath shows better the social development of the
eighteenth century in particular. The story of Beau Nash tells
how the country cousins had to be disciplined to fit into the
fashion, and how swashbuckling had to be put down among
hot-headed young gallants; but Beau Nash could not live for
ever, whereas the stream of social climbers grew ever wider as
scientific progress made more men's fortunes. The novelist
looked on, and coloured history with satire or sly comment.
Smollett and Jane Austen from their different points of view
and different experiences drew pictures of bad manners that
could quite reasonably be true, and the Earl of Chesterfield
warned his son not to learn to play an instrument, as it might
get him into bad company. Here was a difference indeed from
the advice given by Byrd and Morley, though we have seen the
turning-point in Peacham's *The Compleat Gentleman*. Again the
advice is not completely true, for there were plenty of the gentry

who played instruments together in amity and good taste. The individual point of view is comprised of a basic philosophy, partly temperamental, partly educational, and coloured always by experience of life; it throws into relief some particular pattern of the truth, but not the whole of it. All opinions are to some extent wrong, but a collection of different opinions on any subject at any period cannot help but illuminate the tendencies of the time more evenly than any one mind, however great. The Age of Reason could not do away with all the old prejudices, nor were all those who acquired influence at that time worthy of the responsibility it carried. The succeeding age was to profit or suffer accordingly.

Roger North

THE BEGINNING OF MUSICAL ART

IT IS the misfortune of all arts, of which the use happens to be discontinued (leaving no reall specimens, which only can demonstrate what the practice of any such art was, except some dark verball descriptions) and so to fall into the catalogue of the *artes deperditæ*, and be hardly, if ever, recoverable. But yet by some cloudy expression found remaining, to make work for critiques, and the world little the wiser; for arts have peculiar termes, that is, a language understood by the professors, and some few else in the time; but in after times when such arts are attempted to be revived, who should make the Dictionary, or adapt things to the words used by obsolete authors? It is certain that nothing, but the very things appearing by specimens (if any are left) can doe it; and without such authorities, become enigmatick. The mathematical arts have come downe to us intire, because the subject (quantum) is knowne to every body. Rhetorick and poetry bring their proper specimens with them, the old speeches and poems: Architecture but imperfectly, of which the antique is knowne almost intirely by the vestiges yet actually, or in pictures, remaining; and without the help of such the formes of the ancient fabricks had never been gathered out of Vitruvius, who wrote on purpose to instruct them, and is not yet effectually understood.

And this inconvenience hath happened to the science and practice of musick in the highest degree, for among the Greek republicks, that art was held in veneration, as if law, liberty, justice, and morality depended upon it; and the modes and effects of it were the admiration, as well as delight of all men both wise and unwise: and according to the disposition of the philosophers of those times, every naturall energye was moulded to a formall science. So Musick had its fate; and from following nature, and imitation, was made an art with laws and rules not to be enumerated; as they say the adding of a string to an instrument was made almost high treason. And of this subject we have authors upon authors, and commentators upon them. But for want of reall or practicable specimens, it is not understood what their musick was, nor yet by meanes of all the pretended discoverys, can any piece be accordingly framed, that mankind will endure to hear, though Kircher hath vainly attempted it.

I must observe that these assuming Greeks would needs have the originall, and invention of musick, to have arisen amongst them. And for that end wee have poetick relations of dryed nerves in tortoise shells, smith's hammers, and practitioners as Apollo, Orpheus, &c., who might perhaps (as Homer) sing well to a petite instrument at feasts. But I am persuaded that, notwithstanding all these pretensions, Musick had an higher originall, and that is the use of voices, and language among men. And that having such facultys, they must necessarily stumble upon the excercise of what we call singing, that is, pronouncing with an open and extended voice; and however the flexures might be rude at first, in process of time they would improve; especially considering how useful singing was in the pastoritiall life the primitive race of men led; among whom, any one having a clear and good voice, tho' purely naturall, must be a prime musitian;

and perhaps Tuball Cain, or Vulcan, might be such a one, and merit the fame they have had for it.

Memoires of Musick.

Joseph Addison

HANDEL'S OPERAS

Spectatum admissi risum teneatis—HOR.

AN OPERA may be allowed to be extravagantly lavish in its Decorations, as its only Design is to gratifie the Senses, and keep up an indolent Attention in the Audience. Common Sense however requires, that there should be nothing in the Scenes and Machines which may appear Childish and Absurd. How would the Wits of King *Charles's* Time have laughed, to have seen *Nicolini* exposed to a Tempest in Robes of Ermin, and sailing in an open Boat upon a Sea of Paste-Board? What a Field of Raillery would they have been let into, had they been entertain'd with painted Dragons spitting Wild-fire, enchanted Chariots drawn by *Flanders* Mares, and real Cascades in artificial Land-skips? A little Skill in Criticism would inform us, that Shadows and Realities ought not to be mix'd together in the same Piece; and that Scenes, which are designed as the Representations of Nature, should be filled with Resemblances, and not with the Things themselves. If one would represent a wide Champian Country filled with Herds and Flocks, it would be ridiculous to draw the Country only upon the Scenes, and to crowd several Parts of the Stage with Sheep and Oxen. This is joining together Inconsistencies, and making the Decoration partly Real and partly Imaginary. I would recommend what I have here said, to the Directors, as well as to the Admirers, of our Modern Opera.

As I was walking in the Streets about a Fortnight ago, I saw an ordinary Fellow carrying a Cage full of little Birds upon his Shoulder; and, as I was wondering with my self what Use he would put them to, he was met very luckily by an Acquaintance, who had the same Curiosity. Upon his asking him what he had upon his Shoulder, he told him, that he had been buying Sparrows for the Opera. Sparrows for the Opera, says his Friend, licking his lips, what, are they to be roasted? No, no, says the other, they are to enter towards the end of the first Act, and to fly about the Stage.

This strange Dialogue awakened my Curiosity so far, that I immediately bought the Opera, by which means I perceived that the Sparrows were to act the part of Singing Birds in a delightful Grove: though upon a nearer Enquiry I found the Sparrows put the same Trick upon the Audience, that *Sir Martin Mar-all* practised upon his Mistress; for, though they flew in Sight, the Musick proceeded from a Consort of Flagellets and Bird-calls which was planted behind the Scenes. At the same time I made this Discovery, I found by the Discourse of the Actors, that there were great Designs on foot for the Improvement of the Opera; that it had been proposed to break down a part of the Wall, and to surprize the Audience with a Party of an hundred Horse, and that there was actually a Project of bringing the *New-River* into the House, to be employed in Jetteus and Water-works. This project, as I have since heard, is post-poned 'till the Summer-Season; when it is thought the Coolness that proceeds from Fountains and Cascades will be more acceptable and refreshing to People of Quality. In the mean time, to find out a more agreeable Entertainment for the Winter-Season the Opera of *Rinaldo* is filled with Thunder and Lightning, Illuminations and Fire-works; which the Audience may look upon without catching Cold, and indeed without much Danger of being burnt; for there are several Engines filled with Water, and ready to play at a Minute's warning, in case any such Accident should happen. However, as I have a very great Friendship for the Owner of this Theater, I hope that he has been wise enough to *insure* his House before he would let this Opera be acted in it.

It is no wonder, that those Scenes should be very surprizing, which were contrived by two Poets of different Nations, and raised by two Magicians of different Sexes. *Armida* (as we are told in the Argument) was an *Amazonian* Enchantress, and poor Signor Cassani (as we learn from the *Persons Represented*) a Christian-Conjurer (*Mago Christiano*). I must confess I am very much puzzled to find how an *Amazon* should be versed in the Black Art, or how a good Christian, for such is the Part of the Magician, should deal with the Devil.

To consider the Poets after the Conjurers, I shall give you a taste of the *Italian*, from the first Lines of his Preface: *Eccoti, benigno Lettore, un Parto di poche Sere, che se ben nato di Notte, non però aborto di Tenebre, ma si fara conoscere Figlio d' Apollo con qualche Raggio di Parnasso*. *Behold, gentle reader, the Birth of a few Evenings, which, tho' it be the Offspring of the Night, is not the Abortive of Darkness, but will make it self known to be the Son of Apollo, with a certain Ray of Parnassus*. He afterwards proceeds to call Minheer *Hendel* the *Orpheus* of our Age, and to acquaint us, in the same Sublimity of Style, that he Composed the Opera in a Fortnight. Such are the Wits, to whose Tastes we so ambitiously conform our selves. The Truth of it is, the finest Writers among the Modern *Italians* express themselves in such a Florid Form of Words, and such tedious Circumlocutions, as are used by none but Pedants in our own Country; and at the same time fill their Writings with such poor Imaginations and Conceits, as our Youths are ashamed of before they have been two Years at the University. Some may be apt to think that it is the difference of Genius which produces this difference in the Works of the two Nations; but to show there is nothing in this, if we look into the Writings of the old *Italians*, such as *Cicero* and *Virgil*, we shall find that the *English* writers, in their way of thinking and express-ing themselves, resemble these Authors much more than the modern *Italians* pretend to do. And as for the Poet himself, from whom the Dreams of this Opera are taken, I must entirely agree with Monsieur *Boileau*, that one verse in *Virgil* is worth all the *Clincant* or Tinsel of *Tasso*.

But to return to the Sparrows; there have been so many Flights of them let loose in this Opera, that it is feared the House will never get rid of them; and that in other Plays they may make their Entrance in very wrong and improper Scenes, so as to be seen flying in a Lady's Bed-Chamber, or perched upon a King's Throne; besides the Inconveniences which the Heads of the Audience may sometimes suffer from them. I am credibly informed, that there was once a Design of casting into an Opera the Story of *Whittington* and his Cat, and that in order to it there had been got together a great Quantity of Mice; but Mr. *Rich*, the Proprietor of the Play-house, very prudently considered that it would be impossible for the Cat to kill them all, and that consequently the Princes of his Stage might be as much infested with Mice, as the Prince of the Island was before the Cat's Arrival upon it; for which Reason he would not permit it to be Acted in his House. And indeed I cannot blame him; for, as he said very well upon that Occasion, I do not hear that any of the Performers in our Opera pretend to equal the famous Pied Piper, who made all the Mice of a great Town in *Germany* follow his Musick, and by that means cleared the Place of those little Noxious Animals.

Before I dismiss this Paper, I must inform my Reader, that I hear there is a Treaty on foot with *London* and *Wise* (who will be appointed Gardeners of the Play-House) to furnish the Opera of *Rinaldo* and *Armida* with an Orange-Grove; and that the next time it is Acted, the Singing Birds will be personated by Tom-Tits: The Undertakers being resolved to spare neither Pains nor Mony, for the Gratification of the Audience.

The Spectator, Tuesday, March 6, 1711.

Daniel Defoe

THE HOME OF THE CHANDOS ANTHEMS

IT IS in vain to attempt to describe the beauties of this building at Cannons; the whole is a beauty, and as the firmament is a glorious mantle filled with, or as it were made up of a concurrence of lesser glories the stars; so every part of this building adds to the beauty of the whole. The avenue is spacious and majestick, and as it gives you the view of two fronts, join'd as it were in one, the distance not admitting you to see the angle, which is in the centre; so you are agreeably drawn in, to think the front of the house almost twice as large as it really is.

And yet when you come nearer you are again agreeably surprized, by seeing the winding passage opening as it were a new front to the eye, of near 120 feet wide, which you had not seen before, so that you are lost a while in looking near hand for what you so evidently saw a great way off. Tho' many of the palaces in Italy are very large fine buildings, yet I venture to say, not Italy it self can show such a building rais'd from the common surface, by one private hand, and in so little a time as this; For Cannons as I was informed, was not three years a building and bringing the gardens and all, to the most finished beauty we now see it in.

The great palaces of Italy, are either the work of sovereign princes, or have been ages in the building; one family laying the design, and ten succeeding ages and families being taken up, in carrying on the building: But Cannons had not been three years in the Duke's possession, before we saw this prodigy rise out of the ground, as if he had been resolv'd to merit that motto which the French king assum'd, He saw, and it was made.

The building is very lofty, and magnificent, and the gardens are so well designed, and have so vast a variety, and the canals are so large, that they are not to be out done in England; possibly the Lord Castlemain's at Wanstead, may be said to equal but can not exceed them.

The inside of the house is as glorious, as the outside is fine; the lodgings are indeed most exquisitely finish'd, and if I may call it so, royally furnish'd; the chapel is a singularity, not only in its building, and the beauty of its workmanship, but in this also, that the duke maintains there a full choir, and has the worship perform'd there with the best musick, after the manner of the chappel royal, which is not done in any other noble man's chappel in Britain; no not the Prince of Wales, though heir apparent to the throne.

Nor is the chapel only furnish'd with such excellent musick, but the duke has a set of them to entertain him every day at dinner.

The avenues and vistas to this house are extreamly magnificent, the great walk or chief avenue is near a mile in length, planted with two double rows of trees, and the middle walk broad enough for a troop of horse to march in front; in the middle way there is a large basin or fountain of water, and the coaches drive round it on either side; there are three other avenues exceeding fine, but not so very large; the beauty of them all will double, with time, when the trees may be grown, like those of New-Hall, in Essex.

Two things extreamly add to the beauty of this house, namely, the chapel, and the library; but I cannot enlarge, having taken up so much room in the view of this house, as must oblige me to abate in others, to whom I am willing to do what justice I can.

In his gardens and out-houses the duke keeps a constant night-guard, who take care of the whole place, duly walk the rounds, and constantly give the hour to the family at set appointed places and times; so that the house has some waking eyes about it, to keep out thieves and spoilers night and day. In a word, no nobleman in England, and very few in Europe, lives in greater splendour, or maintains a grandeur and magnificence, equal to the Duke of Chandos.

Tour of England and Wales.

Thomas Bisse, D.D.

THE DELIGHTS OF THE SONS OF MEN

"I got me men-singers and women-singers, and the delights of the sons of men, as musical instruments, and that of all sorts."—Eccles. II, 8.

IT PLEASED the Allwise Creator, that as he had made this

inferior World for the use and enjoyment of men, so the wisest of men should make his experiments upon the various happiness it affords: and to the end that all men, inferior in wisdom to judge, or wealth to procure, might be convinced terrestrial happiness was not their ultimate, but that they were designed for better things than these, he has by God's direction written upon this maxim or motto, *"all is vanity and vexation of spirit"*. Yet he had procured to himself all things that are thought magnificent and pleasurable. Thus he enumerates them: "I made me great works, I builded me houses, I planted me vineyards, I made me gardens and orchards, and I planted trees in them of all kind of fruits. I made me pools of water, to water therewith the wood that bringeth forth trees. I got me servants and maidens, and had servants born in my house: also I had great possessions of great and small cattle, above all that were in Jerusalem before me: I gathered me also silver and gold, and the peculiar treasure of kings, and of the provinces:" and then as the close and crown of all, "I got me men-singers and women-singers, and the delights of the sons of men, as musical instruments, and that of all sorts."

Tho' this last kind of happiness be included in the same verdict with the foregoing, and signed with the same inscription, viz. *vanity and vexation;* and if indulged or extended beyond its end, either in our opinion or enjoyment, will prove no better; yet this use may be made of the list or enumeration of human enjoyments as here set down, that Musick is the chief, that this is emphatically above the rest "the delight of the sons of men".

For we find and feel, how by its strange and sympathising energy, it causes love and joy with the dependent train of softer affections to pass through their gradations of warmth and remission, as in a moment. Nay the excess of our passions, which are as so many evil spirits, are subject to its power and ejection. For instance, when anger or grief have got possession of a man, anger attempting to "cast him as into the fire", or grief "as into the water"; yet at the command of musick they have come out of the man, and left him in his right mind. The instance of Saul, in whom the evil spirit was under the controul and expulsion of David's harp, has been often resembled, and in a manner exemplified in human life, and that through all ages and nations. But whence had musick this authority from the beginning, over the natures and degrees of human passions; so as to turn and transform, to cool and comfort, to assuage and heal them, as it listeth, but from nature? And who gave it this authority, this medicinal omnipotence, but the author of nature?

Since then the greatest pleasures of men arise from their passions employed on the objects preordained for them; and since every affection, besides the several enjoyment of its proper object, doth universally delight in harmony, as the common object, enjoyment or relief of all; since this by its addition quickens and multiplies all other enjoyments, and deadens or disperses every adversity; though I am far from affirming, that the Soul is or was made for harmony; yet I cannot affirm less, than that harmony was ordained for man, yea, for the chief among the delights ordained for the sons of men.

And according to this ordinance of nature hath it been made a constant attendant in the greatest scenes of pleasure, in kings' courts, and in the palaces of the mighty. No less hath it born a principal part in Theaters, those fictitious scenes of pleasure, from their first institution; being introduced throughout those entertainments to change the Scenes, and connect the Acts, without which they would have been either insipid or insupportable. What would Tragedy, ancient or modern, be but dull cruelty, without the softening and mitigation of the songs and interludes? and without their exaltation and ornament, Comedy would be but low life in fiction, and often appear under the degeneracy of Farce. Nay, what at present supersede both, our Operas; what are these but a collection of chosen harmony, a concatenation of Songs; which, though composed in an unknown tongue, connected by an unnatural chaunt, upbraided for their irrational half repetition, and for the general futility of the subject and sense, notwithstanding these defects, are for the sake of the harmony, the continued and cardinal entertainments of our Princes, our Nobles, and the chief of our Israel.

Thus then as in Courts and Theaters, singers and musical instruments of all sorts, have been admitted and used for the delights of the sons of men; so have they been also in Temples and Choirs, but then for the delights of the sons of God.

Here I cannot but observe to you, the power which Religion hath over all persons and things, and even over harmony itself; so as by its union or its absence proportionately to affect it, either to increase or evacuate its force, and to double or dissipate its delight. For we know, there are many lovers and admirers of it, that nevertheless have little love or admiration for Church-musick; it becomes to them a dull, dead entertainment, another thing. Part of this alteration may come from nature, part from the force of custom. There are persons of that airy nature and disposition, as to be smitten only with the most light ludicrous airs of the Theatre; [sic] nay, more with the offcasts, extravagances, and intended foils of the Composer, than with his most studied and august *adagios*. I speak not of these, but even of such as sit as master-auditors in Theatres, whose ears examine, enjoy, and exhaust the wonders of the best composition; these theatrical Judges, I say, shall in our Temples sit as foreigners, as hardly understanding and less enjoying the best Choral performances; the songs of Sion are sung to such, as in a strange land.

I own there is and ought to be a great difference, an essential disparity between the compositions formed for the Stage and for the Sanctuary. And the force of custom in our different attendance on them, too often on the one, and too seldom on the other, may create in our relish of them an additional disparity. But yet I take the freedom to ascribe this difference and deficiency of relish to Church-musick partly to an higher, a worse cause, a defect and deadness in religion. For religious persons can enjoy both in their place and proportion. With these too the Theatre has its seasons and pleasures as well as the Temple; but then the greater because of the Temple, and where that has the greatest.

And thus it is in harmony; the musick is not in the instrument, nor in the ear. Only the stroke or motion of the instrument causing a correspondent motion or undulation in the air, and this striking on the ear, and thence the auditory nerves, doth by the law or word of the Creator, raise those delightful sensations in the Soul, we call sounds. The instruments and their furniture, we see, are mere matter, wood, metal, or string, the work of the craftsman; which neither feel, nor hear, nor of themselves move nor send forth any sound. And the ear, though it seems to hear, and is the work of the Divine artificer, is still but an instrument; and though of finer texture and materials than the former, is in itself altogether as insensible. But by the co-operation of both these instruments, natural and artificial, God works in us to hear all we hear and enjoy as musick. "Oh Lord! how wonderful are thy works", and thy continued workmanship by their service in and to us men, and for our delight! That by the reciprocal motions or tremblings of a string or pipe, which we call vibrations, and by the inequality, proportion or coincidence of their number, all the innumerable tones in musick, with their subdivisions, with their discords and symphonies, should take their original. That when the several instruments in consort do by an equal number of vibrations make one sound or unison; yet that each instrument should have its particular sound, and as it were, its own voice; even in equality causing a variety: and all this for the delights of the sons of men.

Oh! that men would therefore praise him for his goodness upon this suitable occasion, and declare the wonders, which in the institution of harmony, and the formation of the objects and instruments in subservience to its enjoyment, I say, declare aloud the wonders that he doth for the children of men! Yea let the heavens, the lofty original pattern of harmony, displayed in their creation, and declared in their revolutions; let the Sun, with the Planets, that mystical Lyre of Apollo with seven chords; let the stars above, let the earth beneath; let every creature that moveth, praise him in their dances; let every thing that soundeth praise him in their songs; *let everything that hath breath*, but us men above all creatures, *praise the Lord*.

> From the Sermon preached at Hereford Cathedral,
> at the Anniversary Meeting of the Three Choirs,
> September 7th, 1726.

Thomas Hearne

AN OPINION OF HANDEL

1733. *July 5th.* One Handel, a foreigner (who, they say, was born at Hanover) being desired to come to Oxford, to perform in Musick this Act, in which he hath great skill, is come down, the Vice-Chancellour (Dr. Holmes) having requested him to do so, and as an encouragement, to allow him the Benefit of the Theater both before the Act begins and after it. Accordingly he hath published Papers for a performance today at 5s. a Ticket. This performance began a little after 5 clock in the evening. This is an innovation. The Players might be as well permitted to come and act. The Vice-Chancellour is much blamed for it. In this, however, he is to be commended for reviving our Acts, which ought to be annual, which might easily be brought about, provided the Statutes were strictly followed, and all such innovations (which exhaust Gentlemen's pockets and are incentives to Lewdness) were hindered.

July 6th. The Players being denied coming to Oxford by the Vice-Chancellour and that very rightly, tho' they might as well have been here as Handel and (his lowsy Crew) a great number of forreign fidlers, they went to Abbington, and yesterday began to act there, at which were present many Gownsmen from Oxford. . . .

Many years ago was printed with wooden cutts Brant's Ship of Fools, translated into English by Alex. Barclay. A supplement should be put to it, containing an account of all those that encouraged Handel & his company last night at our Theater,

and that intend to encourage him when our Act is over. The
Vice-Chancellour is very right to have an Act, but then it should
have been done in statutable way, so as to begin today (the
Encoenia being now reckoned part of the Act) being Friday &
to end next Tuesday morning.

July 8th, Sun. The Professor of Musick (who is Mr. Richard
Goodson) is on the Vespers, by virtue of the Statute, to read an
English Lecture between 9 and 10 Clock in the morning in the
Musick School, with a Consort of Musick also. But yesterday
morning there was nothing done of that, only a little after six
clock or about 7 was a sham consort by Goodson in the Theater,
at which some Ladies were present, but not a soul was pleased,
there being nothing of a Lecture; but this I suppose must go
instead of both a Musick Lecture and a Musick Speech. But
formerly besides the Musick Lecture by the Professor, between
9 and 10 Clock, there used upon Act Monday morning pretty
soon (about 8 Clock) to be an English Musick speech by a distinct
person from the Professor, for the entertainment of the Ladies,
in which were many jocular and satyrical passages, though in
1703 (the year I went out Master) there was nothing of a Musick
Speech, but in 1693 was a very smart biting one. . . .

Half an hour after 5 Clock yesterday in the afternoon was
another Performance, at 5s. a ticket, in the Theater by Mr.
Handel for his own benefit, continuing till about 8 clock.
NB. his book (not worth 1d.) he sells for 1s.

July 11th. In the evening half hour after five o'clock, Handel
and his Company performed again at the Theater, being the
3rd time, at Five shillings a Ticket.

July 12th. Yesterday morning from 9 clock in the morning
till eleven, Handel & his Company performed their Musick in
Christ Church Hall, at 3s. a Ticket.

In the evening of the same day, at half hour after 5, Handel
& his Crew performed again in the Theater at 5s. per Ticket.
This was the fourth time of his performing there.

July 13th. Last night, being the 12th, Handel and his Company
performed again in the Theater, being the 5th time of his per-

forming there, at 5s. per Ticket, Mr. Walter Powel (the Superior Beadle of Divinity) singing, as he hath done all along with them.

July 18*th*. The Prints speak of our late Act at Oxford after the following manner. They observe "that our Public Act began on Friday July 6 with great solemnity. About one o'clock the Rev. Dr. Holmes, President of St. John's College, Vice-Chancellor, together with the several other members of the University in their proper Habits, and a vast concourse of Persons of Distinction of both sexes, repaired to the Theatre, to hear the speeches which were made there by way of Compliment to the King, Queen, Royal Family, and Prince of Orange; also verses on several subjects spoken by young noblemen; and a Dialogue between two scholars, in the Characters of Bellus Homo and Academicus: (which Dialogue was made by Mr. Woodson a schoolmaster in the country, and lately Usher to Mr. Hiley, Schoolmaster at Reading, & spoke by Mr. Baker (now called Bellus Homo) and Mr. Langton, Gentlemen Commomers of Magd. Coll. & lately schoolboys to Mr. Hiley while Woodson was Usher). The evening concluded with Mr. Handel's Oratorio called *Esther*. On Saturday July 7, after seven in the morning, there was a piece of musick performed in the Musick School, and about nine the Lectures in the several other sciences; in the afternoon there were disputations in the (Divinity School, Physick School, Law School and) Theatre, and afterwards an Oratorio. The next day, being Sunday July 8th, Mr. Handel's *Te Deum* and Anthems were performed in St. Mary's Church before a numerous Assembly; and the day after, being Monday, the Exercises in the Theatre were renewed, and a new Oratorio performed called *Athalia*. (This is false, for 'twas not performed till next evening, being Tuesday). The University has been pleased to confer the Degree of Doctor of Laws, on the Right Hon. the Lord Sidney Beauclerk, but Mr. Handel has not accepted his Degree of Doctor of Musick, as was reported, that Gentleman having declined the honour, when tendered him at Cambridge. There was a very great appearance of Ladies at all the publick Entertainments, and the Town very full of Company." This is the substance of the Prints of Monday July 16, as the Publishers received their Account from Oxford.

The Prints also, dated from London the 12th inst., say farther, that they write from Oxford, that on Monday July 9th, the Theatre was again crowded with Nobility, Gentry &c. of both sexes, to hear the Disputations continued when seven doctors in Divinity, eight of Physick, several of the Civil Law, and eighty-four Masters of Arts were created with the usual ceremony ... and the next night (being Tuesday) another *Oratorio* of Mr. Handel's called *Athalia*, was performed in the Theatre, where 3,700 Persons were present. ...

And moreover from London of the 14th being Saturday 'tis noted that 'twas computed, that Mr. Handel cleared by his Musick at Oxford upwards of 2,000*l*.

1734, *April 28th.* In the Convocation Wed. last, Apr. 24, when the new Proctors were admitted, a letter was read from Lord Arran, our Chancellor, that there might be no Act this year, 1734. It was carried accordingly by a small majority, that there shall be none. The Vice-Chancellour, Dr. Holmes, it seems, hath had enough of Acts, and that made him send for a letter, otherwise had not he sent for one, there had been one of course. The mad impudent method last Act of bringing a parcel of Pickpockets hither, to run away with the money, shocked all understanding men, who wished there might be no Acts, unless they were carried on in a statutable way, as 'twas hoped for the future he would, and that therefore this Vice-Chancellour would have begun this very year 1734 to have reduced it to the statutable method, but it appears now, that it hath been judged most convenient to have none, it being pretended to put it off (which is old threadbare reason) that there are no Doctors, which however is a poor reason, it being certain that there are always Masters or Doctors of Arts, and some exercises might be done, let the number of Artists &c. be never so few.

Remarks and Collections of Thomas Hearne.

Philip Dormer Stanhope, Fourth Earl of Chesterfield

PATERNAL ADVICE

DEAR BOY,

This letter will, I believe, still find you at Venice, in all the dissipation of masquerades, ridottos, operas, &c.: with all my heart; they are decent evening amusements, and very properly succeed that serious application to which I am sure you devote your mornings. There are liberal and illiberal pleasures as well as liberal and illiberal arts. There are some pleasures that degrade a gentleman as much as some trades do. Sottish drinking, indiscriminate gluttony, driving coaches, rustic sports, such as fox-chases, horse-races, &c., are, in my opinion, infinitely below the honest and industrious professions of a tailor and a shoemaker, which are said to *déroger*.

As you are now in a musical country, where singing, fiddling, and piping are not only the common topics of conversation, but almost the principal objects of attention; I cannot help cautioning you against giving in to those (I will call them illiberal) pleasures, (though music is commonly reckoned one of the liberal arts,) to the degree that most of your countrymen do when they travel in Italy. If you love music, hear it; go to operas, concerts, and pay fiddlers to play to you; but I insist upon your neither piping nor fiddling yourself. It puts a gentleman in a very frivolous, contemptible light; brings him into a great deal of bad company; and takes up a great deal of time, which might be much better employed. Few things would mortify me more, than to see you bearing a part in a concert, with a fiddle under your chin, or a pipe in your mouth.

I have had a great deal of conversation with Comte du Perron, and Comte Lascaris, upon your subject; and I will tell you, very truly, what Comte du Perron (who is, in my opinion, a very pretty man) said of you. *Il a de l'esprit, un scavoir peu commun à son age, une grande vivacité, et quand il aura pris des manières il sera parfait; car il faut avouer qu'il sent encore le collége; mais cola viendra.* I was very glad to hear, from one whom I think so good a judge, that you wanted nothing but *des manières;* which I am convinced you will now soon acquire in the company which henceforwards you are likely to keep. But I must add, too, that, if you should not acquire them, all the rest will be of very little use to you. By *manières,* I do not mean bare common civility; everybody must have that, who would not be kicked out of company: but I mean engaging, insinuating, shining manners; a distinguished politeness, an almost irresistible address; a superior gracefulness in all you say and do. It is this alone that can give all your other talents their full lustre and value; and, consequently, it is this which should now be the principal object of your attention. Observe minutely, wherever you go, the allowed and established models of good-breeding, and form yourself upon them. Whatever pleases you most, in others, will infallibly please others, in you. I have often repeated this to you; now is your time of putting it in practice.

Pray make my compliments to Mr. Harte; and tell him I have received his letter from Vienna, of the 16th N.S., but that I shall not trouble him with an answer to it, till I have received the other letter, which he promises me, upon the subject of one of my last. I long to hear from him after your settlement at Turin: the months that you are to pass there will be very decisive ones for you. The exercises of the Academy, and the manners of Courts, must be attended and acquired, and, at the same time, your other studies continued. I am sure you will not pass, nor desire, one single idle hour there; for I do not foresee that you can, in any part of your life, put out six months to greater interest, than those next six at Turin.

We will speak hereafter about your stay at Rome, and in other parts of Italy. This only I will now recommend to you; which is, to extract the spirit of every place you go to. In those places, which are only distinguished by classical fame, and valuable remains of antiquity, have your Classics in your hand and in your head: compare the ancient geography, and descriptions, with the modern; and never fail to take notes. Rome will furnish you with business enough of that sort; but then it furnishes you with many other objects well deserving your attention, such as deep ecclesiastical craft and policy. Adieu!

Letter to his son, dated from London, April 19, O.S., 1749.

Tobias Smollett

WELCOME TO BATH

THREE DAYS ago we came hither from the Hot Well, and took possession of the first floor of a lodging-house on the South Parade; a situation which my uncle chose, for its being near the bath, and remote from the noise of carriages. He was scarce warm in the lodging, when he called for his night-cap, his wide shoes and flannel, and declared himself invested with the gout in his right foot; though, I believe, it had as yet reached no farther than his imagination. It was not long before he had reason to repent his premature declaration; for our aunt Tabitha found means to make such a clamour and confusion, before the flannels could be produced from the trunk, that one would have imagined the house was on fire. All this time, uncle sat boiling with impatience, biting his fingers, throwing up his eyes, and muttering ejaculations; at length he burst into a kind of convulsive laugh, after which he hummed a song; and, when the hurricane was over, exclaimed, "Blessed be God for all things!" This, however, was but the beginning of his troubles. Mrs. Tabitha's favourite dog Chowder, having paid his compliments to a female turnspit, of his own species, in the kitchen, involved himself in a quarrel with no fewer than five rivals, who set upon him at once, and drove him up stairs to the dining-room door, with hideous noise: There our aunt and her woman, taking arms in his defence, joined the concert, which became truly diabolical.

This fray being with difficulty suppressed, by the intervention of our own footman and the cook-maid of the house, the squire had just opened his mouth to expostulate with Tabby, when the town-waits, in the passage below, struck up their music (if music it may be called) with such a sudden burst of sound, as made him start and stare, with marks of indignation and disquiet. He had recollection enough to send his servant with some money, to silence those noisy intruders; and they were immediately dismissed, though not without some opposition on the part of Tabitha, who thought it but reasonable that he should have more music for his money. Scarce had he settled this knotty point when a strange kind of thumping and bouncing was heard right overhead in the second storey, so loud and violent as to shake the whole building. I own I was exceedingly provoked at this new alarm; and, before my uncle had time to express himself on the subject, I ran up stairs, to see what was the matter. Finding the room-door open, I entered without ceremony, and perceived an object, which I cannot now recollect without laughing to excess— it was a dancing master, with his scholar, in the act of teaching. The master was blind of one eye, and lame of one foot, and led about the room his pupil, who seemed to be about the age of threescore, stooped mortally, was tall, raw-boned, hard-favoured, with a woollen nightcap on his head; and he had stript off his coat, that he might be more nimble in his motions.

Finding himself intruded upon by a person he did not know, he forthwith girded himself with a long iron sword, and advancing to me, with a peremptory air, pronounced, in a true Hibernian accent, "Mister What-d'ye-callum, by my shoul and conscience I am very glad to sea you, if you are after coming in the way of friendship; and indeed, and indeed now, I believe you are my friend sure enough, gra; though I never had the honour to sea your face before, my dear; for because you come like a friend without any ceremony at all, at all"—I told him the nature of my visit would not admit of ceremony; that I was come to desire he would make less noise, as there was a sick gentleman below, whom he had no right to disturb with such preposterous doings. "Why, look ye now, young gentleman", replied this original, "perhaps, upon another occason, I might shivilly request you to explain the maining of that hard word, *pre-pasterous:* But there's a time for all things, honey"—So saying, he passed me with great agility, and, running downstairs, found our footman at the dining-room door, of whom he demanded admittance, to pay his respects to the stranger. As the fellow did not think proper to refuse the request of such a formidable figure, he was immediately introduced, and addressed himself to my uncle in these words: "Your humble servant, good sir,— I am not so *prepasterous*, as your son calls it, but I know the rules of shivility—I'm a poor knight of Ireland, my name is Sir Ulic Mackilligut, of the County of Galway; being your fellow-lodger, I'm come to pay my respects, and to welcome you to the South Parade, and to offer my best services to you, and your good lady, and your pretty daughter; and even to the young gentleman your son, though he thinks me a *prepasterous* fellow— You must know I am to have the honour to open a ball, next door, tomorrow, with Lady Macmanus; and, being rusted in my dancing, I was refreshing my memory with a little exercise; but if I had known there was a sick person below, by Christ! I would sooner have danced a hornpipe upon my own head, than walked the softest minuet over yours."

My uncle, who was not a little startled at his first appearance, received his compliment with great complacency, insisted upon his being seated, thanked him for the honour of his visit, and reprimanded me for my abrupt expostulation with a gentleman of his rank and character. Thus tutored, I asked pardon of the knight, who, forthwith starting up, embraced me so close, that I could hardly breathe; and assured me, he loved me as his own soul. At length, recollecting his nightcap, he pulled it off in some confusion; and, with his bald pate uncovered, made a thousand apologies to the ladies, as he retired.

At that instant, the Abbey bells began to ring so loud, that we could not hear one another speak; and this peal, as we afterwards learned, was for the honour of Mr. Bullock, an eminent cow-keeper of Tottenham, who had just arrived at Bath, to drink the waters for indigestion. Mr. Bramble had not time to make his

remarks upon the agreeable nature of this serenade, before his
ears were saluted with another concert that interested him more
nearly. Two negros that belonged to a Creole gentleman, who
lodged in the same house, taking their station at a window in the
staircase, about ten feet from our dining-room door, began to
practise upon the French-horn; and, being in the very first
rudiments of execution, produced such discordant sounds, as
might have discomposed the organs of an ass.—You may guess
what effect they had upon the irritable nerves of uncle; who,
with the most admirable expression of splenetic surprise in his
countenance, sent his man to silence these dreadful blasts, and
desire the musicians to practise in some other place, as they had
no right to stand there, and disturb all the lodgers in the house.
Those sable performers, far from taking the hint, and withdrawing, treated the messenger with great insolence, bidding him
carry his compliments to their master Colonel Rigworm, who
would give him a proper answer, and a good drubbing into the
bargain: In the meantime they continued their noise, and even
endeavoured to make it more disagreeable, laughing between
whiles, at the thoughts of being able to torment their betters
with impunity. Our squire, incensed at the additional insult,
immediately dispatched the servant with his compliments to
Colonel Rigworm, requesting that he would order his blacks
to be quiet, as the noise they made was altogether intolerable.

To this message the Creole colonel replied, that his horns had
a right to sound on a common staircase; that there they should
play for his diversion; and that those who did not like the noise
might look for lodgings elsewhere. Mr. Bramble no sooner
received this reply, than his eyes began to glisten, his face grew
pale, and his teeth chattered. After a moment's pause, he slipt
on his shoes without speaking a word, or seeming to feel any
farther disturbance from the gout in his toes. Then snatching his
cane, he opened the door, and proceeded to the place where the
black trumpeters were posted. There, without farther hesitation,
he began to belabour them both; and exerted himself with such
astonishing vigour and agility, that both their heads and horns

were broken in a twinkling, and they ran howling down stairs
to their master's parlour-door. The squire, following them half
way, called aloud, that the colonel might hear him, "Go, rascals,
and tell your master what I have done; if he thinks himself
injured, he knows where to come for satisfaction. As for you,
this is but an earnest of what you shall receive, if ever you presume
to blow a horn again here, while I stay in the house." So saying,
he retired to his apartment, in expectation of hearing from the
West Indian; but the colonel prudently declined any farther
prosecution of the dispute. My sister Liddy was frightened into
a fit, from which she no sooner recovered than Mrs. Tabitha
began a lecture upon patience; which her brother interrupted
with a most significant grin, exclaiming, "True, sister, God
increase my patience and your discretion. I wonder", added he,
"what sort of sonata we are to expect from this overture, in
which the devil that presides over horrid sounds hath given us
such variations of discord.—The trampling of porters, the
creaking and crashing of trunks, the snarling of curs, the scolding
of women, the squeaking and squalling of fiddles and hautboys
out of tune, the bouncing of the Irish baronet overhead, the
bursting, belching, and brattling of French horns in the passage,
(not to mention the harmonious peal that still thunders from the
Abbey steeple,) succeeding one another without interruption,
like the different parts of the same concert, have given me such
an idea of what a poor invalid has to expect in this temple,
dedicated to silence and repose, that I shall certainly shift my
quarters tomorrow, and endeavour to effectuate my retreat before
Sir Ulic opens the ball with my Lady Macmanus, a conjunction
that bodes me no good."

The Expedition of Humphry Clinker

James Boswell

SENSE IN LITERATURE AND MUSIC

ON TUESDAY, September 23, (1777) Johnson was remarkably

cordial to me. It being necessary for me to return to Scotland soon, I had fixed on the next day for my setting out, and I felt a tender concern at the thought of parting with him. He had, at this time, frankly communicated to me many particulars, which are inserted in this work in their proper places; and once, when I happened to mention that the expense of my jaunt would come to much more than I had computed, he said, "Why, Sir, if the expense were to be an inconvenience, you would have reason to regret it: but, if you have had the money to spend, I know not that you could have purchased as much pleasure with it in any other way."

During this inteview at Ashbourne, Johnson and I frequently talked with much pleasure of mere trifles which had occurred in our tour to the Hebrides; for it had left a most agreeable and lasting impression upon his mind.

He found fault with me for using the phrase to *make* money. "Don't you see (said he) the impropriety of it? To *make* money is to *coin* it: you should say *get* money." The phrase, however, is, I think, pretty current. But Johnson was at all times jealous of infractions upon the geniune English language, and prompt to repress colloquial barbarisms; such as, *pledging myself*, for *undertaking; line*, for *department*, or *branch*, as, the *civil line*, the *banking line*. He was particularly indignant against the almost universal use of the word *idea* in the sense of *notion* or *opinion*, when it is clear that the *idea* can only signify something of which an image can be formed in the mind. We may have an *idea* or *image* of a mountain, a tree, a building; but we cannot surely have an *idea* or *image* of an *argument* or *proposition*. Yet we hear the sages of the law "delivering their *ideas* upon the question under consideration;" and the first speakers in parliament "entirely coinciding in the *idea* which has been ably stated by an honourable member;"—or "reprobating an *idea* unconstitutional, and fraught with the most dangerous consequences to a great and free country." Johnson called this "modern cant".

I perceived that he pronounced the word *heard*, as if spelt with a double *e*, *heerd*, instead of sounding it *herd*, as is most usually done. He said, his reason was, that if it was pronounced *herd*, there would be a single exception from the English pronunciation of the syllable *ear*, and he thought it better not to have that exception.

In the evening our gentleman-farmer, and two others, entertained themselves and the company with a great number of tunes on the fiddle. Johnson desired to have "Let ambition fire thy mind", played over again, and appeared to have a patient attention to it; though he owned to me that he was very insensible to the power of musick. I told him, that it affected me to such a degree, as often to agitate my nerves painfully, producing in my mind alternate sensations of pathetick dejection, so that I was ready to shed tears; and of daring resolution, so that I was inclined to rush into the thickest part of the battle. "Sir said he, I should never hear it, if it made me such a fool."

Much of the effect of musick, I am satisfied, is owing to the association of ideas. That air, which instantly and irresistibly excites in the Swiss, when in a foreign land, the *maladie du pais*, has, I am told, no intrinsick power of sound. And I know from my own experience, that Scotch reels, though brisk, make me melancholy, because I used to hear them in my early years, at a time when Mr. Pitt called for soldiers "from the mountains of the north", and numbers of brave Highlanders were going abroad, never to return. Whereas the airs in *The Beggar's Opera*, many of which are very soft, never fail to render me gay, because they are associated with the warm sensations and high spirits of London. This evening, while some of the tunes of ordinary composition were played with no great skill, my frame was agitated, and I was conscious of a generous attachment to Dr. Johnson, as my preceptor and friend, mixed with an affectionate regret that he was an old man, whom I should probably lose in a short time. I thought I could defend him at the point of my sword. My reverence and affection for him were in full glow. I said to him, "My dear Sir, we must meet every year, if you don't quarrel with me." JOHNSON, "Nay, sir, you are more likely to quarrel

I

with me, than I with you. My regard for you is greater almost than I have words to express; but I do not choose to be always repeating it; write it down in the first leaf of your pocket-book, and never doubt of it again."

Life of Johnson

Oliver Goldsmith

OLIVIA'S ELOPEMENT

AS I only studied my child's real happiness, the assiduity of Mr. Williams pleased me, as he was in easy circumstances, prudent, and sincere. It required but very little encouragement to revive his former passion; so that in an evening or two he and Mr. Thornhill met at our house, and surveyed each other for some time with looks of anger; but Williams owed his landlord no rent, and little regarded his indignation. Olivia, on her side, acted the coquette to perfection, if that might be called acting which was her real character, pretending to lavish all her tenderness on her new lover. Mr. Thornhill appeared quite dejected at this preference, and with a pensive air took leave, though I own it puzzled me to find him so much in pain as he appeared to be, when he had it in his power so easily to remove the cause, by declaring an honourable passion. But whatever uneasiness he seemed to endure, it could easily be perceived that Olivia's anguish was still greater. After any of these interviews between her lovers, of which there were several, she usually retired to solitude, and there indulged her grief. It was in such a situation I found her one evening, after she had been for some time supporting a fictitious gaiety.—"You now see, my child", said I, "that your confidence in Mr. Thornhill's passion was all a dream: he permits the rivalry of another, every way his inferior, though he knows it lies in his power to secure you to himself by a candid declaration."—"Yes, papa", returned she, "but he has his reasons for this delay: I know he has. The sincerity of his looks and words convinces me of his real esteem. A short time, I hope, will discover the generosity of his sentiments, and convince you that my opinion of him has been more just than yours." —"Olivia, my darling", returned I, "every scheme that has been hitherto pursued to compel him to a declaration, has been proposed and planned by yourself, nor can you in the least say that I have constrained you. But you must not suppose, my dear, that I will ever be instrumental in suffering an honest rival to be the dupe of your ill-placed passion. Whatever time you require to bring your fancied admirer to an explanation shall be granted; but at the expiration of that term, if he is still regardless, I will absolutely insist that honest Mr. Williams shall be rewarded for his fidelity. The character which I have hitherto supported in life demands this from me, and my tenderness as a parent, shall never influence my integrity as a man. Name then your day, let it be as distant as you think proper, and in the meantime take care to let Mr. Thornhill know the exact time on which I design delivering you up to another. If he really loves you, his own good sense will readily suggest that there is but one method alone to prevent his losing you for ever."—This proposal, which she could not avoid considering as perfectly just, was readily agreed to. She again renewed her most positive promise of marrying Mr. Williams, in case of the other's insensibility; and at the next opportunity, in Mr. Thornhill's presence, that day month was fixed upon for her nuptials with his rival.

Such vigorous proceedings seemed to redouble Mr. Thornhill's anxiety: but what Olivia really felt gave me some uneasiness. In this struggle between prudence and passion, her vivacity quite forsook her, and every opportunity of solitude was sought, and spent in tears. One week passed away; but Mr. Thornhill made no efforts to restrain her nuptials. The succeeding week he was still assiduous; but not more open. On the third he discontinued his visits entirely, and instead of my daughter testifying any impatience, as I expected, she seemed to retain a pensive tranquility, which I looked upon as resignation. For my own part,

I was now sincerely pleased with thinking that my child was going to be secured in a continuance of competance and peace, and frequently applauded her resolution, in preferring happiness to ostentation.

It was within about four days of her intended nuptials, that my little family at night were gathered round a charming fire, telling stories of the past, and laying schemes for the future. Busied in forming a thousand projects, and laughing at whatever folly came uppermost, "Well, Moses", cried I, "we shall soon, my boy, have a wedding in the family; what is your opinion of things and matters in general?"—"My opinion, father, is, that all things go on very well; and I was just now thinking, that when sister Livy is married to farmer Williams, we shall then have the loan of his cyder-press and brewing-tubs for nothing."—"That we shall, Moses", cried I, "and he will sing us *Death and the Lady*, to raise our spirits into the bargain".—"He has taught that song to our Dick", cried Moses, "and I think he goes through it very prettily".—"Does he so?" cried I, "then let us have it: where's little Dick? let him up with it boldly."— "My brother Dick", cried Bill my youngest, "is just gone out with sister Livy; but Mr. Williams has taught me two songs, and I'll sing them for you papa. Which song do you choose, *The Dying Swan*, or *The Elegy on the Death of a Mad Dog*?" "The elegy, child, by all means", said I; "I never heard that yet; and Deborah, my life, grief you know is dry, let us have a bottle of the best gooseberry wine, to keep up our spirits. I have wept so much at all sorts of elegies of late, that without an enlivening glass, I am sure this will overcome me; and Sophy, love, take your guitar and thrum in with the boy a little."

AN ELEGY ON THE DEATH OF A MAD DOG

Good people all of every sort,
   Give ear unto my song,
And if you find it wond'rous short,
   It cannot hold you long.

In Islington there was a man,
　　Of whom the world might say,
That still a godly race he ran,
　　When'er he went to pray.

A kind and gentle heart he had,
　　To comfort friends and foes;
The naked every day he clad,
　　When he put on his clothes.

And in that town a dog was found,
　　As many dogs there be,
Both mongrel, puppy, whelp, and hound,
　　And curs of low degree.

This dog and man at first were friends;
　　But when a pique began,
The dog, to gain some private ends,
　　Went mad and bit the man.

Around from all the neighbouring streets
　　The wondering neighbours ran,
And swore the dog had lost his wits,
　　To bite so good a man.

The wound it seemed both sore and sad
　　To every Christian eye;
And while they swore the dog was mad,
　　They swore the man would die.

But soon a wonder came to light,
　　That showed the rogues they lied,
The man recovered of the bite,
　　The dog it was that dy'd.

"A very good boy, Bill, upon my word, and an elegy that may truly be called tragical. Come, my children, here's Bill's health, and may he one day be a bishop."

"With all my heart" cried my wife; and if he but preaches as well as he sings, I make no doubt of him. The most of his family, by the mother's side, could sing a good song: it was a common saying in our country, that the family of the Blenkinsops could never look straight before them, nor the Hugginsons blow out a candle; that there were none of the Grograms but could sing a song, or of the Marjorams but could tell a story."—"However that be", cried I, "the most vulgar ballad of them all generally pleases me better than the fine modern odes, and things that petrify us in a single stanza; productions that we at once detest and praise. Put the glass to your brother, Moses. The great fault of these elegiasts is, that they are in despair for griefs that give the sensible part of mankind very little pain. A lady loses her muff, her fan, or her lap-dog, and so the silly poet runs home to versify the disaster."

"That may be the mode", cried Moses, "in sublimer compositions; but the Ranelagh songs that come down to us are perfectly similar, and all cast in the same mould: Colin meets Dolly, and they hold a dialogue together; he gives her a fairing to put in her hair, and she presents him with a nosegay; and then they go together to church, where they give good advice to nymphs and swains to get married as fast as they can."

"And very good advice too", cried I, "and I am told there is not a place in the world where advice can be given with so much propriety as there; for, as it persuades us to marry, it also furnishes us with a wife; and surely that must be an excellent market, my boy, where we are told what we want, and supplied with it when wanting."

"Yes, sir", returned Moses, "and I know but of two such markets for wives in Europe—Ranelagh in England, and Fontarabia in Spain. The Spanish market is open once a year, but our English wives are saleable every night."

"You are right, my boy", cried his mother, "Old England is the only place in the world for husbands to get wives"—"And for wives to manage their husbands", interrupted I. "It is a proverb abroad, that if a bridge were built across the sea, all the ladies of the Continent would come over to take pattern from ours; for there are no such wives in Europe as our own. But let us have one more bottle, Deborah, my life, and Moses give us a good song. What thanks do we not owe to Heaven for thus bestowing tranquility, health, and competence. I think myself happier now than the greatest monarch upon earth. He has no such fireside, nor such pleasant faces about it. Yes, Deborah, we are now growing old; but the evening of our life is likely to be happy. We are descended from ancestors that knew no stain, and we shall leave a good and virtuous race of children behind us. While we live they will be our support and our pleasure here, and when we die they will transmit our honour untainted to posterity. Come, my son, we wait for a song: let us have a chorus. But where is my darling Olivia? That little cherub's voice is always sweetest in a concert."

Just as I spoke Dick came running in, "O papa, papa, she is gone from us, she is gone from us, my sister Livy is gone from us for ever!"—"Gone, child!"—"Yes, she is gone off with two gentlemen in a post-chaise, and one of them kissed her, and said he would die for her; and she cried very much, and was for coming back; but he persuaded her again, and she went into the chaise, and said, 'O what will my poor papa do when he knows I am undone!' "—"Now then", cried I, "my children, go and be miserable; for we shall never enjoy one hour more. And O may Heaven's everlasting fury light upon him and his! Thus to rob me of my child! And sure it will, for taking back my sweet innocent that I was leading up to heaven. Such sincerity as my child was possessed of! But all our earthly happiness is now over! Go, my children, and be miserable and infamous; for my heart is broken within me!"—"Father", cried my son, "is this your fortitude?"—"Fortitude, child! Yes, he shall see I have fortitude! Bring me my pistols. I'll pursue the traitor. While he is on earth I'll pursue him. Old as I am, he shall find I can sting him yet. The villain! The perfidious villain!"

The Vicar of Wakefield, Ch. XVII

Dr. Charles Burney

THE CASTRATI

THERE SEEM to have been no *singing eunuchs* in antiquity, unless we allow the Galli, or Archigalli, priests of Cybele, to be such; who, in imitation of Atys, the favourite of that goddess, mutilated themselves at their initiation, and used to sing extempore songs, and play on instruments through the streets.

Castration has, however, at all times been practised in Eastern countries to furnish jealousy and tyranny with *safe-guards* to female chastity; yet never, as I have been able to ascertain, merely to preserve the voice for the vain amusement of the public, till about the latter end of the sixteenth century. But although I detest the perpetrators of such horrid crimes against human nature as the parents commit, who sacrifice that tenderness which every other part of creation manifests for its offspring, in order to gratify avarice or ambition; yet I cannot subscribe to the common assertion that *Evirati are all cowards, devoid of genius* for literature, or any solid study; and that even the voice, for the melioration of which they are so inhumanly treated, is inferior to that of a woman or boy.

With respect to the operation affecting the mind so much as to deprive it of all fortitude in times of danger, there is great reason to doubt the fact: most of the generals of Eastern monarchs having been at all times of this class; and the bravest stand that ever was made against Alexander the Great, was at Gaza, under the command of one of Darius's generals, who was a eunuch. Ammianus Marcellinus gives an account of Menophilus, a eunuch, to whom Mithridates entrusted his daughter, which proves the possibility of such unfortunate persons possessing a heroism equal to that of the most determined Stoic. I think Guadagni and Pacchierotti were so far from timid and pusillanimous, that they would *seek* danger rather than *shun* it, if called upon or irritated.

As to genius, I never found those of the first class in Music deficient in intellectual abilities for more serious studies. Indeed, I have seen *real* genius and disposition for literary pursuits, in more than one great opera singer; and as for composition, and the theory of Music, not only the *best singers* of the Pope's Chapel ever since the beginning of the last century, but the *best composers* are among the *soprani*, in that service.

Prejudice has been carried so far as to say, that an *Evirato* is unable to utter the letter *r;* indeed, if an Italian, he will not perhaps snarl that letter in so canine a manner as some French and English singers do, perhaps to show their manhood; but defect of elocution is no more peculiar to eunuchs, than to any other part of the human species.

I shall now return to Della Valle's account of singers in Italy from the beginning of the sixteenth century to the year 1640, when he wrote his *Discourse.* After saying he had been present at the performance of the first oratorio in Rome; he tells us, that the style of singing began to improve from that time; and at present, says he, we have Nicolini, Bianchi, Giovannini, Lorenzini, Mario, and many others, who not only equal, but surpass the singers of more early times, at least in taste and judgment.—"But let us quit the consideration of all other voices, and speak only of *sopranos*, the greatest ornaments of Music. You are pleased," he says to his friend, "to compare the *falsetti* of former times with the *soprani*, which at present are so common? but who ever sung then like a Guidobaldo, a Cavalier Loreto, a Gregorio, an Angeluccio, a Marc-Antonio, and many more that might be named? The best resource then was a boy, with a good voice; but boys, the instant they begin to know their business, lose their voices, and it is allowed, even while they remain in their greatest perfection, that their performance, on account of their youth and inexperience, must inevitably be devoid of taste, judgment, and grace; indeed, it is generally so mechanical and unfeeling, that I hardly ever heard a boy sing without receiving more pain than pleasure. The *soprani* of the present times, being, on the contrary, persons of mature age and judgment, sing with such science, expression, and taste, as to ravish every hearer of sensibility. During the last age there was no such singer, except Padre Soto, and afterwards, Girolamo, who is still living.

At present every court and every chapel in Italy is furnished with them; and besides *Evirati*, what age could boast of so many excellent female singers?" Here he celebrates the talents of a great number, who had been high in favour at Florence and elsewhere, both for dramatic and chamber singing, but particularly at Rome. In speaking of these, he asks "who hears without rapture Signora Leonora sing to her own accompaniment on the arch-lute, which she touches in so fanciful and masterly a manner? And who will now venture to say, which is the best performer, she, or her sister Caterina? nor is there one who, like me, has seen and heard Signora Adriana, their mother, when, during her youth, she sailed in a felucca, near the Pausilippan grotto, with her golden harp in her hand, but must confess that in our times, these shores were inhabited by Sirens, that are not only beautiful and tuneful, but virtuous and beneficent." He praises likewise Signora Maddalena with her sister, who were called the Lolle, and were the first he heard sing well at Rome, after his return from the Levant; and Signor(a) Sofonisba, who a few years before had as great applause in Rome, as ever was given to any one in the ancient theatre of Marcellus. After celebrating the talents of several others, who were living at the time of his writing, he mentions la Francesca Caccini, by the Tuscans called la Cecchina, daughter of the famous Giulio Caccini Romano, who had been many years the admiration of Florence, where he heard her himself in his youth, not only for her musical abilities both in singing and composition, but for her poetry both in the Latin and Tuscan language. He then speaks of the nuns of his time, as exquisite singers, particularly la Verovia, and others, *Nello Spirito Santo* at Rome, who for many years had astonished the world: the nuns of Santa Lucia in Silici, as well as the nuns of San Silvestro, of Magnanopoli, and Santa Chiara, whom people flock to hear as miraculous. In short, he concludes, that such was the number and excellence of the singers of his time, that those who were not content with their performance, must certainly be either too fond of antiquity, as is usual with old people; or too fastidious and unwilling to be pleased; which proceeds from affectation, and a pretence to more taste and delicacy than other people, or from a nausea, resembling that of persons in sickness, who want appetite for the most exquisite dainties.

A General History of Music, Vol. 4, Ch. 1

Richard Brinsley Sheridan

ENTER LORD FOPPINGTON

Lord Foppington. Dear Loveless, I am your most humble servant.

Loveless. My lord, I'm yours.

Lord Fop. Madam, your ladyship's very obedient slave.

Love. My lord, this lady is a relation of my wife's.

Lord Fop (Salutes Berinthia). The beautifullest race of people on earth, rat me! Dear Loveless, I am overjoyed that you think of continuing here: I am, stap my vitals!—(*To Amanda*) For Gad's sake, madam, how has your ladyship been able to subsist thus long, under the fatigue of a country life?

Aman. My life has been very far from that, my lord; it has been a very quiet one.

Lord Fop. Why, that's the fatigue I speak of, madam; for 'tis impossible to be quiet without thinking: now thinking is to me the greatest fatigue in the world.

Aman. Does not your lordship love reading, then?

Lord Fop. Oh, passionately, madam; but I never think of what I read. For example, madam, my life is a perpetual stream of pleasure, that glides through with such a variety of entertainments, I believe the wisest of our ancestors never had the least conception of any of 'em. I rise, madam, when in tawn, at twelve o'clock. I don't rise sooner, because it is the worst thing in the world for the complexion: nat that I pretend to be a beau; but a man must endeavour to look decent, lest he makes so odious a figure in the side-bax, the ladies should be compelled to turn their eyes upon the play. So at twelve o'clock, I say, I rise. Naw, if it is a good day, I resalve to take the exercise of riding; so drink my chocolate, and draw on my boots by two. On my return, I dress; and, after dinner, lounge perhaps to the opera.

Ber. Your lordship, I suppose, is fond of music?

Lord Fop. Oh, passionately, on Tuesdays and Saturdays[1] for then there is always the best company, and one is not expected to undergo the fatigue of listening.

Aman. Does your lordship think that the case at the opera?

Lord Fop. Most certainly, madam. There is my Lady Tattle, my Lady Prate, my Lady Titter, my Lady Sneer, my Lady Giggle, and my Lady Grin—these have boxes in the front, and while any favouite air is singing, are the prettiest company in the waurld, stap my vitals!—Mayn't we hope for the honour to see you added to our society, madam?

Aman. Alas! my lord, I am the worst company in the world at a concert, I'm so apt to attend to the music.

Lord Fop. Why, madam, that is very pardonable in the country or at church, but a monstrous inattention in a polite assembly. But I am afraid I tire the company?

Love. Not at all. Pray go on.

Lord Fop. Why then, ladies, there only remains to add, that I generally conclude the evening at one or other of the clubs; not that I ever play deep; indeed I have been for some time tied up from losing above five thousand pounds at a sitting.

Love. But isn't your lordship sometimes obliged to attend the weighty affairs of the nation?

Lord Fop. Sir, as to weighty affairs, I leave them to weighty heads; I never intend mine shall be a burden to my body.

Ber. Nay, my lord, but you are a pillar of the state.

Lord Fop. An ornamental pillar, madam; for sooner than undergo any part of the fatigue, rat me, but the whole building should fall plump to the ground!

[1] Tuesdays and Saturdays were opera nights.

Aman. But, my lord, a fine gentleman spends a great deal of his time in his intrigues; you have given us no account of them yet.

Lord Fop (*Aside*). So! she would enquire into my amours—that's jealousy, poor soul!—I see she's in love with me.—(*Aloud*) O Lord, madam, I had like to have forgot a secret I must need tell your ladyship.—Ned, you must not be so jealous now as to listen.

Love (*Leading Berinthia up the stage*). Not I, my lord; I am too fashionable a husband to pry into the secrets of my wife.

Lord Fop (*Aside to Amanda, squeezing her hand*). I am in love with you to desperation, strike me speechless!

Aman (*Strikes him on the ear*). Then thus I return your passion.—An impudent fool!

Lord Fop. God's curse, madam, I am a peer of the realm!

A Trip to Scarborough, Act II, Sc. i.

Sir John Hawkins

CRITICISM

DR. BOYCE had no sooner acquitted himself of his engagements to the public in the above instance, than he gave another direction to his studies. Mr. Garrick had, some years before, employed him to compose a Dirge for the funeral procession in *Romeo and Juliet*, another for the play of *Cymbeline*, and other songs for the theatre, and being now about to revive *The Winter's Tale* he got him to contribute his aid to that performance by setting the songs: Dr. Boyce readily undertook the task, and succeeded very happily in it, particularly in that pleasant dialogue for three voices between Autolycus and his two sweethearts, *Go you hence for I must go*, in which with singular ingenuity he has expressed the humour of Shakespeare in a melody, the gayest and most natural that can be conceived.

Before this time the instrumental music of the theatres, Vauxhall, and other places of resort, had consisted chiefly of the concertos of Corelli, Geminiani, and Martini, and the overtures of Mr. Handel: these last had, for many years, served for the first music or prelude to plays and were grown so familiar, that the country dances, *Greensleeves*, and *Sir Roger de Coverley* were not better known and more common with the vulgar than the gavot in *Otho*, the minuet in *Rodelinda*, and that in *Ariadne*. At this crisis, Dr. Boyce had lying by him, the new-years' and birthday odes which he had composed during the time he had filled the station of master of the royal band. The overtures to these he thought would be well received, and, about the year 1770, he published twelve of them. They are very original and spirited compositions, and abound with elegant airs, and the evidences of deep skill and learned ingenuity.

The taste of the people at the time of the publication of these, was very unpropitious to their success; they had the misfortune to meet with the compositions of Bach and Abel which had already gotten possession of the public ear. Those two persons had the patronage of the late Duke of York, who himself was a proficient on the violoncello; the style they introduced was void of the chief excellencies of music, it was coarse and artless; their basses had no melody, but were tediously monotonous, and to the eye resembled a row of pins.

Bach and Abel were nevertheless eminent musicians, especially the former, who in the composition of an oratorio of Metastasio entitled *Gioas*, performed at the Haymarket to a thin audience, gave proof of his great abilities; but like most of that profession who are to live by the favour of the public, both he and Abel had two styles of composition, the one for their own private delight, the other for the gratification of the many.

Yet these, too, had their fate; the multifarious productions of Bach and Abel, their *Trios*, *Quartettos*, and *Quintettos*, as they are called, together with their *Periodical Overtures*, were heard, and consigned to oblivion; but their style of writing in a great measure survives. We no more hear the solemn and pathetic *Adagio*, the artful and well-studied *Fugue*, or the sweet modulations of the keys with the minor third: all is *Allegro* and *Prestissimo*, and, if not discord, such harmony as the ear sickens at hearing. Such music Mr. Handel was used to listen to and laugh at, and comparing it to a game of cards, would exclaim "Now D is trumps now A," in allusion to those vulgar transitions from the key note to its fifth, with which such sort of music, especially when accompanied with French horns, abounds.

Having thus experienced the vitiated taste of the public, Dr. Boyce abandoned the thought of giving to the world any more of his works, and so deeply rooted in him was this resolution, that being once prest by the writer of these memoirs, to follow the example of Croft and Greene, who had each of them published a collection of anthems, the one of thirty and the other of forty, his answer was, that he was contented his should remain in the church books, and that he would never more solicit the aid of a subscription to enable him to publish what might fail of being well received.

To the above account of his studies, a sketch of his moral character may be thought not an improper adjunct. He possessed a great degree of that modesty peculiar to real artists, arising from a comparison of their works with their ideas, and the inferiority of the former to the latter, that rendered him ever indifferent to applause and even commendation. He declined composing an anthem on occasion of his present Majesty's coronation, to the words "Zadok the Priest, &c.", alledging that it would be presumption in him to attempt it after Mr. Handel; his excuse was accepted, and he made one to other words, which was performed. He had composed a three-part song to the words, "'Tis on earth the greatest blessing", printed in Hales *Social Harmony* with the foolish title of *The Mystic Bower*, and adapted to a panegyric on Free-Masonry. This composition, a friend of his once took occasion to commend, saying it was nearly equal to Blow's *Go, perjured man*. Boyce was offended at the comparison, said it deserved not to be named at the same time as that fine song, and accused his friend of insincerity and a desire to flatter him. He was endowed with the qualities of truth, justice, and integrity, was mild and gentle in his deportment, above all resentment against such as envied his reputation, communicative of his knowledge, sedulous and punctual in the discharge of the duties of his several employments, particularly those that regarded the performance of divine service, and in every relation of life a worthy man.

Memoir of Dr. Boyce in the second edition of Boyce's *Cathedral Music.*

Fanny Burney (Madam D'Arblay)

A DAUGHTER'S COMMENT

Saturday, January 6th, 1787. Today arrived again my dearest father, in consequence of the gracious speeches that had passed about his lengthened stay when here last. Sweet, hospitable Mrs. Delany received him; but he came to me to dinner,—at the Queen's suggestion. Miss P— and Miss Planta were of our party; Mrs. Delany could only join us at coffee.

This evening proved indeed a pleasant one; the honours paid my dear father gladdened my heart. The King came into my room to see Mrs. Delany, and conversed with him so openly, so gaily, and so readily, that it was evident he was pleased with his renewed visit, and pleased with his society. Nor was this all; soon after, the Queen herself came also, purposely to see him. She immediately sat down, that she might seat Mrs. Delany, and then addressed herself to my father, with the most winning complacency. Repeatedly, too, she addressed herself to me, as if to do me honour in my father's eyes, and to shew him how graciously she was disposed towards me. I had previously entreated my father to snatch at any possible opportunity of expressing his satisfaction in all that related to me, as I knew it would not only give pleasure to her benevolence, but was a token of gratitude literally expected from him.

My Susan, however, knows our dear father, and will know

him by the following trait: he had planned his speech, and was quite elevated with the prospect of making it, and with the pleasure of my pointing it out, and being so happy! Dearest father! how blessed in the facility of believing all people as good and as happy as he wishes them! Nevertheless, no sooner did the King touch upon that dangerous string, the history of music, than all else was forgotten! Away flew the speech,—the Queen herself was present in vain,—eagerly and warmly he began an account of his progress, and an enumeration of his materials,— and out from his pockets came a couple of dirty books, which he had lately picked up, at an immense price, at a sale, and which, in shewing to the King, he said were equally scarce and valuable, and added, with energy, "I would not take fifty pounds for that!" Just as if he had said—little as he meant such meaning— "Don't hope for it to your own collection!"

Was not this a curious royal scene?

Diary and Letters of Madame D'Arblay

Charles Dibdin

DIGNITY AND IMPUDENCE

FROM MEN who are ill-informed and of low manners, it is not extraordinary that I should be addressed in a style of authoritative ignorance. Thus I was not at all surprised that the Mayor of Nottingham should ask me if I came with drums and trumpets, and whether I was sure my entertainment would not corrupt the apprentice boys; but I have always considered it as a most pitiable circumstance that the vice-chancellor of a university should so desert his own consequence, and so forfeit his title to that philanthropy, for which his calling ought in a peculiar manner to qualify him, as to entertain an ignorant and mean suspicion of a stranger, and treat him as a rank imposter, even when he had incontrovertible testimony to the contrary; but I will relate the circumstance as it happened.

The person I allude to was Dr. Elliston, who, in the year 1787, was vice-chancellor of Cambridge; and, as a conversation I had with that divine will serve as an illustration of that fact which I mean to bring before the public, I shall give it literally.

"Sir, I have the honour to introduce myself to you. My name is Dibdin. I come to Cambridge with the intention of offering the University a little musical entertainment, which has given great satisfaction in other places, and particularly at Oxford, where I had the vice-chancellor's permission."

"Ha! you had the vice-chancellor's permission at Oxford, had you? How do I know that?"

"I assure you, Sir, upon my honour, I had; however, as I am a perfect stranger, you are certainly not obliged to credit me on my bare assertion, therefore, please look at these letters."

I then produced a letter from Dr. Hayes, and another from Dr. Chapman, both of which corroborated the the fact I had stated.

"Ah, well this letter gives you leave, to be sure, but it does not say that your entertainment is such a one as ought to be delivered at a university."

"It is true, Sir, Dr. Chapman never saw the entertainment in question, not even to this moment, but he was kind enough to suppose I would not offend against the etiquette of that university of which he is such an ornament, or commit such an outrage on propriety as to offer its members any thing unworthy of the patronage, through which I had the honour to appear before them; and to convince me he was of that opinion, Mrs. Chapman, and several ladies with her, attended the performance; nay, Sir, to show you beyond contradiction that the amusement obtained the good opinion of the University in general, here is a paragraph in the Oxford paper, announcing, that at the particular request of many respectable members of the different colleges, the vice-chancellor extended the permission in consequence of the satisfaction I had given."

"Oh, the paragraph in the paper is nothing at all; a man put a paragraph in the Cambridge paper the other day, about me, and it was all a lie."

"Sir, Mr. Jackson, who prints the Oxford paper, is a man of probity and fortune; he idolizes the vice-chancellor, and could not be induced, for any consideration, to use his name to grace a falsity."

"Upon my word you speak very well; one may easily see by your conversation you have merit."

"I am obliged to you, Sir, for your good opinion."

"But you see the morals of the young men are in my care, and as Dr. Chapman never saw the entertainment, he may yet be imposed upon. I have seen your bill, and I think it holds out something immoral. Besides, if you are a man of this reputation, what can induce you to come strolling about the country?"

"Sir, I am going to India, and as I wish, before my departure, to bid adieu to a generous public, who have afforded me a long and liberal patronage——"

"Why, do you know any body at Cambridge?"

"No, Sir."

"Then it is plain the people here do not make any part of that public, to whom you are so much obliged, consequently they have no right to be thanked. Thus you see, as you are rich enough to come with no other motive than mere gratitude, why pay it where it is not due?"

"Good God, Sir, am I obliged to know all those who wish me well as a public man?"

"Well, Sir, I know not what to say. It has always been my rule to give no permission, to one who is not recommended by someone belonging to the University. You say you know nobody."

"I have brought a letter for Dr. Randall."

"Oh, Dr. Randall won't do."

"What sort of person must it be, Sir."

"Why, for instance, a fellow-commoner of one of the colleges."

"I have a letter to a gentleman so described in my pocket. It is unsealed, please read it, Sir. He is, unfortunately, not at Cambridge; but you can readily believe that, upon the strength of his friend's recommendation, he would have waited on you with pleasure."

"It does not signify, Sir, the gentleman is not here to speak for himself, and I cannot credit mere appearances."

"Sir, had I known there would have been so many difficulties thrown in the way of a request which it would have done you neither dishonour nor discredit to grant, I would not have given myself a moment's trouble about it."

"Oh, Sir, if you begin to talk of difficulties, I have done."

"So would I, Sir, did I not feel a little hurt at being deprived, by your suspicions, of giving Cambridge an amusement that has been so followed at Oxford."

"My suspicions, Sir?"

"Yes, Sir, for you must suppose me a most impudent impostor, after every thing that has happened."

"Well, but surely you are not the Mr. Dibdin who composed *The Padlock*, and such a number of musical works?"

"I am, Sir, and I am sorry you could not prevail on yourself to believe it sooner."

"Why, really, this, to be sure, alters the case."

"In short, Sir, as this conversation has imperceptibly stolen on thus far, I am determined you shall be convinced. The Duke of Grafton, as I take it, is Chancellor of Cambridge; you are only Vice-chancellor, and I am sure I know a channel through which I can get you his Grace's recommendation of me."

"Why now, upon my word, this is a strange mistake; pray sit down."

"I beg to be excused, Sir."

"I am sorry a constant rule which I prescribe myself in these cases should occasion such a misunderstanding. You may perform, Sir, on Monday."

This being the very point I wanted to bring him to, I abruptly wished him a good morning, and he followed me to the door with many apologies, of which I took no manner of notice. As soon as I got to my lodging I prepared to write the following letter which I took care should be delivered as expeditiously as possible:

Sir,

When I did myself the honour in a letter to the Vice-Chancellor of Oxford, to thank him for a similar favour to that which I this day requested of you, I could not help noticing that the manner of conferring a kindness, constituted incomparably before all other considerations, its value. You, Sir, with a vigilent zeal, no doubt, for the interest of morality, have thought proper to disbelieve what that gentleman saw no rational cause to discredit; yet, let me assure you, that the letters from Dr. Hayes and Dr. Chapman were not forgeries; the paragraph in the Oxford paper was no fabrication to deceive you; the letter to Mr. Thomson, of Trinity College, was really written by a man of fortune; and I declare I did not, in a single instance, misrepresent or exaggerate any circumstance. Lest, however, you should think this letter, as well as the rest, an imposition, I hasten to the purpose for which it was written, and inform you, that I take the liberty to decline that permission you have so very liberally granted.

I am, Sir, &c.,

C. Dibdin

June 10, 1787.

The Professional Life of Mr. Dibdin, written by himself.

Jane Austen
A PARTY AT LADY CATHERINE'S

COLONEL FITZWILLIAM'S manners were very much admired at the Parsonage, and the ladies all felt that he must add considerably to the pleasure of their engagements at Rosings. It was some days, however, before they received any invitation thither; for while there were visitors in the house, they could not be necessary; and it was not till Easter-day, almost a week after the gentlemen's arrival, that they were honoured by such an attention, and then they were merely asked on leaving church to come there in the evening. For the last week they had seen very little of either Lady Catherine or her daughter. Colonel Fitzwilliam had called at the Parsonage more than once during the time, and Mr. Darcy they had only seen at church.

This invitation was accepted, of course, and at a proper hour they joined the party in Lady Catherine's drawing-room. Her ladyship received them civilly, but it was plain that their company was by no means so acceptable as when she could get nobody else; and she was, in fact, almost engrossed by her nephews, speaking to them, especially to Darcy, much more than to any other person in the room.

Colonel Fitzwilliam seemed really glad to see them: anything was a welcome relief to him at Rosings; and Mrs. Collins's pretty friend had moreover caught his fancy very much. He now seated himself by her, and talked so agreeably of Kent and Hertfordshire, of travelling and staying at home, of new books and music, that Elizabeth had never been half so well entertained in that room before; and they conversed with so much spirit and flow as to draw the attention of Lady Catherine herself, as well as Mr. Darcy. His eyes had been soon and repeatedly turned towards them with a look of curiosity; and that her ladyship, after a while, shared the feeling was more openly acknowledged, for she did not scruple to call out—

"What is that you are saying, Fitzwilliam? What is it you are talking of? What are you telling Miss Bennet? Let me hear what it is."

"We were speaking of music, madam", said he, when no longer able to avoid a reply.

"Of music! Then pray speak aloud. It is of all subjects my delight. I must have my share in the conversation, if you are speaking of music. There are few people in England, I suppose, who have more true enjoyment of music than myself, or a better natural taste. If I had ever learnt, I should have been a great proficient. And so would Anne, if her health had allowed her to apply. I am confident that she would have performed delightfully. How does Georgiana get on, Darcy?"

Mr. Darcy spoke with affectionate praise of his sister's proficiency.

"I am very glad to hear such a good account of her", said Lady Catherine; "and pray tell her from me that she cannot expect to excel if she does not practise a great deal."

"I assure you, madam", he replied, "that she does not need much advice. She practises very constantly."

"So much the better. It cannot be done too much; and when I write next to her, I shall charge her not to neglect it on any account. I often tell young ladies that no excellence in music is to be acquired without constant practise. I have told Miss Bennet several times that she will never play really well unless she practises more; and though Mrs. Collins has no instrument, she is very welcome, as I often told her, to come to Rosings every day, and play on the pianoforte in Mrs. Jenkinson's room. She would be in nobody's way, you know, in that part of the house."

Mr. Darcy looked a little ashamed of his aunt's illbreeding, and made no answer.

When coffee was over, Colonel Fitzwilliam reminded Elizabeth of having promised to play to him, and she sat down directly to the instrument. He drew a chair near her. Lady Catherine listened to half a song, and then talked, as before, to her other nephew; till the latter walked away from her, and moving with his usual deliberation towards the pianoforte, stationed himself so as to command a full view of the fair performer's countenance. Elizabeth saw what he was doing, and, at the first convenient pause, turned to him with an arch smile, and said—

"You mean to frighten me, Mr. Darcy, by coming in all this state to hear me. But I will not be alarmed, though your sister does play so well. There is a stubbornness about me that never can bear to be frightened at the will of others. My courage always rises with every attempt to intimidate me."

"I shall not say you are mistaken", he replied, "because you could not really believe me to entertain any design of alarming you; and I have had the pleasure of your acquaintance long enough to know that you find great enjoyment in occasionally professing opinions which in fact are not your own."

Elizabeth laughed heartily at this picture of herself, and said to Colonel Fitzwilliam, "Your cousin will give you a very pretty notion of me, and teach you not to believe a word I say. I am particularly unlucky in meeting with a person so well able to expose my real character in a part of the world where I had hoped to pass myself with some degree of credit. Indeed, Mr. Darcy, it is very ungenerous in you to mention all that you knew to my disadvantage in Hertfordshire—and, give me leave to say, very impolitic too—for it is provoking me to retaliate, and such things may come out as will shock your relations to hear."

"I am not afraid of you", said he, smilingly.

"Pray let me hear what you have to accuse him of", cried Colonel Fitzwilliam. "I should like to know how he behaves amongst strangers."

"You shall hear, then; but prepare for something very dreadful. The first time of my ever seeing him in Hertfordshire, you must know, was at a ball; and at this ball, what do you think he did? He danced only four dances! I am sorry to pain you, but so it was. He danced only four dances! though gentlemen were scarce; and, to my certain knowledge, more than one young lady was sitting down in want of a partner. Mr. Darcy, you cannot deny the fact."

"I had not at that time the honour of knowing any lady in the assembly beyond my own party"'

"True; and nobody can ever be introduced in a ballroom. Well, Colonel Fitzwilliam, what do I play next? My fingers wait your orders."

"Perhaps", said Darcy, "I should have judged better, had I sought an introduction; but I am ill-qualified to recommend myself to strangers."

"Shall we ask your cousin the reason of this?" said Elizabeth, still addressing Colonel Fitzwilliam. "Shall we ask him why a man of sense and education, and who has lived in the world, is ill-qualified to recommend himself to strangers?"

"I can answer your question", said Fitzwilliam, without applying to him. "It is because he will not give himself the trouble."

"I certainly have not the talent which some people possess", said Darcy, "of conversing easily with those I have never seen before. I cannot catch their tone of conversation, or appear interested in their concerns, as I often see done."

"My fingers", said Elizabeth, "do not move over this instrument in the masterly manner which I see so many women's do. They have not the same force or rapidity, and do not produce the same expression. But then I have always supposed it to be my own fault, because I would not take the trouble of practising. It is not that I do not believe my fingers as capable as any other woman's of superior execution."

Darcy smiled and said, "You are perfectly right, You have employed your time much better. No one admitted to the privilege of hearing you can think anything wanting. We neither of us perform to strangers."

Here they were interrupted by Lady Catherine, who called out to know what they were talking of. Elizabeth immediately began playing again. Lady Catherine approached, and, after listening for a few minutes, said to Darcy—

"Miss Bennet would not play at all amiss if she practised more, and could have the advantage of a London master. She has a very good notion of fingering, though her taste is not equal to Annie's. Annie would have been a delightful performer had her health allowed her to learn."

Elizabeth looked at Darcy to see how cordially he assented to his cousin's praise; but neither at that moment nor at any other could she discern any symptom of love; and from the whole of his behaviour to Miss de Bourgh she derived this comfort for Miss Bingley, that he might have been quite likely to marry *her* had she been his relation.

Lady Catherine continued her remarks on Elizabeth's performance, mixing with them many instructions on execution and taste. Elizabeth received them with all the forbearance of civility, and, at the request of the gentlemen, remained at the instrument till her ladyship's carriage was ready to take them all home.

Pride and Prejudice, Chapter 31.

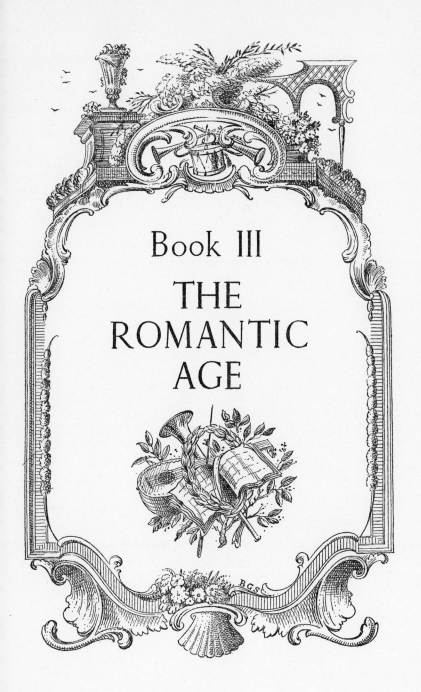

Book III

THE ROMANTIC AGE

THE ROMANTIC AGE

IN 1765 Bishop Percy saw a servant lighting his fire with some sheets from a manuscript collection of ballads. He rescued the remainder of the collection, and these formed the basis of his published work called *Reliques of Ancient Poetry*. This book had an influence greater than its compiler might have expected, for it attracted the attention of cultured Germans, who were led thereby to take an increased interest in English literature. The great age of Goethe and Schiller in German literature set a high regard for Shakespeare in that country, and Goethe himself had a great admiration for Oliver Goldsmith's *The Vicar of Wakefield*. Indeed, on so high a pedestal did they put the British at this time, that we are tempted to look for some explanation outside the realm of the arts. It is most likely that admiration of the British in Germany at the end of the eighteenth century and the beginning of the nineteenth century, came as a reaction to the domination of France. The Revolution in France disturbed the thought of all Europeans, and the aggressive tactics of Napoleon made matters worse. England had openly condemned the Revolution, and thinking Germans felt drawn towards this country, where it seemed that loyalty to human rights stood paramount to political interests. The Germans did not consider American opinion as closely as they might have done, or their views would have changed. America, in any case, was sympathetic towards French thought. The essential policy for the salvation of Germany as an independent nation was philosophic and artistic, since the country was politically subjugated; but the thought of the intellectual Germans was highly subjective, so much so that ideals and interpretations of facts became mixed to a remarkable extent.

Consider the effect of marching Highlanders on the impressionable Goethe:

> "They all carried their heads so freely and gallantly, and stepped so lightly along with their strong bare legs, that it seemed as if there were no original sin, and no ancestral failing, so far as they were concerned."

The picture is admirable: the comment is pure fancy.

Yet this quality of subjective interpretation of natural behaviour formed the basis of German romantic art of the nineteenth century, and it is one of the greatest periods of all art. In music Schubert and Loewe paid tribute to Percy's *Reliques of Ancient Poetry* by setting to music German poems that had their origin in Percy's collection. Loewe's setting of the ballad of *Edward* is a good example, and Schubert's *The Erl King*. Wordsworth, Byron, Coleridge, and Scott wrote romantic tales and poems; these in turn inspired continental musical works—*Rob Roy* and *Lucia di Lammermoor* in opera, *Mazeppa* in a symphonic poem, and as might be expected, Shakespeare was much used as a literary foundation for both these forms as the nineteenth century went on. Broadly speaking it may be said that though the English language carried much of the early romantic thought to fruition, English musicians accepted the supremacy of continental composers, and persistently paid court to foreigners. Even with our ballads, which had had so much to do with romantic inspiration abroad, we were seriously concerned only with the words.

Yet between the words and the music of ballads there was a union that did much to stabilise form. The tunes remained fairly constant through the ages, while new words were always being made up to be sung to popular tunes. A battle, a political disturbance, a crime, or a surprising love-match—any of these things would be a new theme for a ballad. Set against the background of everyday life some unusual event stood out in contrast, and this contrasting theme was the point of appeal. All good storytelling has been of this nature from time immemorial. A delight

in everyday things—in nature and the history of familiar places—
offered scope to the new story-tellers: Sir Walter Scott used
English history for the background to his novels, but it was
always secondary to his imagination. His novels, however,
though not always historically correct, are often illuminating,
for he could depict effectively and economically the motives of
his characters through their behaviour in matters of taste. In
Old Mortality the spirit of the Covenanters is thrown into contrast
with that of the English troops by Scott's description of the brave
challenge of the soldiers' trumpets, answered by the metrical
psalmody of the Scottish resisters. One can well understand the
appeal such stories made to musicians, for such scenes are the
very essence of musical drama. Here is romanticism at its best,
before its stamina was sapped by sickly sentimentality.

Less well known to continental musicians, however, were the
writings of the early nineteenth century English essayists.
William Hazlitt was a dramatic critic drawn into consideration
of opera because it was one of the attractions of the stage, and his
friend Charles Lamb wrote an essay entitled *A Chapter on Ears*
wherein he makes the confession that music is a torture to him.
Yet this essay is one of the most penetrating commentaries on
the psychology of music that the nineteenth century writers
produced. Lamb understands the force of musical expression,
though he is unable to follow its context. "I have been practising
God Save the King all my life; whistling and humming it over to
myself in solitary corners; and am not yet arrived, they tell me,
within many quavers of it. Yet hath the loyalty of Elia never
been impeached." Far better that one should write like this—
truly and with conviction—than that one should write like
R. D. Blackmore, who in *Lorna Doone* had a "clarionet" to
accompany a village choir singing an *Exmoor Harvest-Song* in the
seventeenth century. (The clarinet came to England in the middle
of the eighteenth century). A lack of understanding of music
among authors may have prevented some of them from intro-
ducing this art into their novels in the nineteenth century, but
the age was not unmusical; music was passionately sought by all

classes of society. Lamb is very conscious of his loss: "It is hard to stand alone in an age like this", he says, "constituted to the quick and critical perception of all harmonious combinations, I verily believe, beyond all preceding ages."

In spite of this Hazlitt has some hard things to say about the behaviour of artists and audiences at the opera. People chattered in the gallery, and appeared in the boxes for the sake of fashion. He does not like Braham, whom Weber said was "the greatest singer in Europe", because Braham liked to exploit his own personality. Hazlitt is hard, but fair: would that all musical criticism in the nineteenth century had been equally so. He struck out at the real evil that beset the art of opera in England, which was its financial arrangements. Singers could command high fees, and to some extent dictate terms if sufficiently famous, but the real controllers of opera were the managers. The nineteenth century saw a long line of these gentlemen in charge of the Italian Opera in London. They paid high fees to principal singers, but cut expenditure to the bone on everything else; the result can be imagined from a report by Hazlitt published in *The Champion* on August 14th, 1814.

"Nothing could be more unpleasant than the impression produced on our minds by the exhibition of Saturday last. Tattered hanging fragments of curtains, disjointed machinery, silver panels turned black, a few thinly scattered lamps badly lighted, were among the various circumstances which threw a damp over our spirits. Bankruptcy everywhere stared us in the face. The general *coup d'œil* of the theatre had no affinity with gaiety or grandeur. The whole had the melancholy appearance, without any of the sublimity, of some relic of Eastern magnificence."

Of the various managers, few knew much about music: they were business men, and if their autobiographies are to be believed, shady ones. Gone were the days when composers like Handel managed their own opera productions. Not until 1830 was there any change for the better, and that came with the appointment of a young Italian, Michael Costa, as *maestro al cembalo* (i.e., conductor-pianist). Costa had sufficient force of personality to weld the various elements of opera at Covent Garden into something resembling a whole, and he gained the approval of the public for his more satisfactory performances; as a result of this he was able to bring some pressure to bear on the management, but certainly not enough to swing London into line with the Continent in opera production.

The fight between artistic standards and financial control had an interesting phase in the year 1828, when the committee of the Philharmonic Society of London decided that the funds of that Society should be divided amongst their members' families, in proportion as the members died off. It was argued that as the Society had been built up through their care and attention, it would be unfair to let later generations reap the benefit. Such a decision was quite opposed to the rules of the Society, as laid down by its founders; these rules stated that the object of the Society was to further the cause of good orchestral music in London, and that members had no personal claim on these funds. Publicity prevented the proposed division of spoils taking place, but it must have been rather a shock to the committee in an age when the cause of private profit was so sacred, to find that public opinion could overrule their decision. Artistic standards could be fought for in such a Society, but in a purely business concern such arguments would have little weight. The London pleasure gardens declined through false economies, as we can tell from Charles Dickens' description of *Vauxhall Gardens by Day* in *Sketches by Boz*. (That must have been between 1834 and 1836). Another ten years and the music was of the lowest order, and the dancing as bad, or worse, than that at Greenwich Fair described in *Sketches by Boz*. Cheeseparing reduced the entertainments to starvation point, like the fowls Dickens describes in *Vauxhall Gardens by Day*, and so the golden eggs got fewer; finally they ceased to be laid.

Another change was taking place in the taste of the audiences.

They were losing the flexibility that had obtained in the eighteenth century. Previously musical novelties had been expected, but now audiences tended only to accept recognised favourite compositions, and new compositions were expected to be in an easily-recognised style. Handel was first favourite in the concert-room, with Mendelssohn an acceptable modernist. The classical symphonists were applauded, and Mozart had a good appeal as a writer of operas; so had Rossini and the other light Italian and French opera composers. Ballet was popular, indeed too popular, for operas were often cut to make room for long ballets in as many as six acts. In the midst of this there was little room for more serious opera, and though it has been maintained by a French critic, Augustin Filon, that the gradual decay of the London theatres from about 1840 was due to a fondness for music, critics could grow very hot on occasion when a new opera appeared. The *Musical World* on June 8th, 1850, reprinted a report that had previously appeared in the *Morning Post*: it was entitled *Verdi at the Italian Opera*.

"A great uproar took place at this establishment last night; several persons attired in quaint costumes appeared on the stage, and for some reasons which we in vain endeavoured to make out from the business of the scene, or the requirements of the dramatic action, uttered strange cries and piercing screams. The strain upon their pulmonic resources appeared to be very great indeed, yet on the whole *they* did their duty manfully. After ruminating for some time at these peculiar proceedings, and searching deeply for the philosophy of this vocal raving, we were at length fortunate enough to lay this before our readers, not as a conclusive solution of the problem, but simply as a proposition which may, perhaps, afford a clue to the mystery.

Verdi, the hope of young Italy—Verdi, whose music (?) is being performed with success throughout musical Europe, and is the admiration of many Italian vocalists, must needs possess some wondrous excellence. Musicians (the poor

162

blind creatures!) may not be able to discover it, they may not be able to discern in it any of those attributes of musician-ship which they worship in Mozart and other dull writers of the so-called classical school; but musicians are seldom philoso-phers, and Verdi is—hence his incomprehensible superiority, and the great difference which exists between him and all other great composers. Verdi's style may in a great measure be considered as a tremendous musical illustration of the popular maxim that "unity is power"; but his chief and noblest aim appears to be to show that the human voice, when strained to the utmost, can be made to produce more noise than any combination of instruments whatever, to assert the supremacy of the "voice of Nature", to prove its superiority over mere mechanical inventions and contrivances, even though they are made of brass or sheepskin. Who can deny the elevation of this purpose? Nature versus Art! Why should man or woman be outroared by an ugly trombone, or outscreamed by an impertinent octave-flute?

To the great object we have mentioned, Verdi has devoted his energies; in the pursuit of it, all smaller considerations to which unphilosophical composers have given their atten-tion, such as melody, harmony, counterpoint, dramatic propriety, originality, &c., have appeared to him insignificant and unworthy the attention of a genius."

Again there is self-deception. Verdi was no philosopher, but the reference to the phrase "Unity is Power" would lead Englishmen of 1850 to think of Trade-Unionism, Chartism, and internal dissention; Verdi however was an Italian patriot, and his countrymen looked to their national art of opera for express-ion of their wish for freedom, but this wish was for national freedom—freedom from the yoke of foreign rule. England had no such problem. This strange misconception is then turned to account in pure artistic criticism, and used to deride Verdi's greater use of the orchestra than his fellow Italian composers, and his more powerful use of the solo voice. Characteristic is the writer's assumed criterion of Mozart for all opera: it was in keeping with the thought of 1850.

This is but one of the shams that we now recognise in mid-Victorian opinion: More obvious to us is their besetting sin of nostalgia. At the beginning of the century Charles Lamb could refer to Burton's *Anatomy of Melancholy* and show how music affected him with the symptoms Burton had described, but this is not sentimentality. Consider on the other hand Mrs. Sheppard's novel *Charles Auchester*. The literary style of this book was praised by no less a person than Disraeli. Why, it is difficult to say today, for great tracts of the book are in an artificial diction that we should call pretentious. To make matters worse, these parts of the book would be the most interesting to us if they were not so obvious a sham. Mrs. Sheppard was a great admirer of Mendelssohn, and a character in *Charles Auchester* named Seraphael may actually be an idealised portrait of Mendelssohn; but what a portrait! Sentimental hero-worship of the lushest kind, and this all because the authoress feels she ought to excel herself in depicting the man. It is when she drops to the level of simple characters that Mrs. Sheppard is at her best. Idealisation is still there, but a revealing idealisation that could—and did—make for improvement in the lives of the Victorians. The description of Lenhart Davey's cottage, so trim and neat, so cultured in its atmosphere, yet achieved despite the handicap of small means, is a Victorian conception of goodness that embraced both beauty and truth. Truth not in the beginning, but in the working-out of the ideal, for there were people of humble means who, through a love of music and a wish to spend themselves in making musical the lives of others, earned the esteem of their neighbours and created for themselves little havens in the midst of squalor and ugliness. They were valuable in furthering the cause of the great musical festivals that grew in number as the nineteenth century ran its course. The neglect of these festivals by social historians is a curious oversight; they are remarkable for having toned down religious distinctions and class distinctions at a time when there was much open enmity in the cities.

One aspect of this is shown in Disraeli's novel *Sybil, or the Two Nations*, wherein there is an authentic picture of a scene rarely described by Victorian writers without moral comment. There in a single chapter the drink trade jostles with the temperance movement, and the temperance movement with trade unionism, and trade unionism with the tricks of employers, all through the thoughts of different characters met together in a Victorian super-tavern. The whole place breathed art—reeked of it. Round the walls were paintings of scenes from the most romantic tales in English literature, and a lady in a white robe on the stage, with a golden harp, together with a fiddler with a black moustache, pretending to be very superior artists. Social superiority in low life—the very essence of Victorian ambition. "'You never were here before; its the only place. That's the Lady of the Lake', he added, pointing to a picture; 'I've seen her at the circus, with real water.'" Uplift. Profitable too. Let us not look with too great a contempt on the proprietor of "The Temple of the Muses" (alias "The Cat and Fiddle") for there are other scenes that could be described, in public-houses that had no music, and the incidents in these would show that popular contemporary play *Ten Nights in a Bar-room* to be a highly moral exhibition. There was so much self-deception in everything the Victorians preached, that we are sometimes held amazed at their apparent audacity. It was Charles Kingsley (not Karl Marx) who first denounced the use of religion as a social narcotic: "We have used the Bible as if it were a mere special constable's handbook, an opium dose for keeping beasts of burden patient while they are being overloaded", but it is nevertheless possible to read sermons where Kingsley preached the harmony of law and order with a nostalgic explanation of music as a pattern and type of heaven, mixed with some simple remarks on what we might now call musical appreciation. The fact is that some Victorians were frightened of society as they knew it: they escaped in romantic dreams that seemed to them beautiful and not untrue. In 1861 a musical clergyman, the Rev. H. R. Haweis, came out in defence even of the Christy Minstrels:

"The negro mind, at work upon civilized music, produces the same kind of thing as the negro mind at work upon Christian theology. The product is not to be despised. . . . If we could divest ourselves of prejudice, the songs that float down the Ohio river are one in feeling and character with the songs of the Hebrew captives by the waters of Babylon. We find the same tale of bereavement and separation, the same irreparable sorrow, the same simple faith and childlike adoration, the same wild tenderness and passionate sweetness, like music in the night."

Childlike adoration indeed! "Happy shall he be that taketh and dasheth thy little ones against the stones." What would the audience of a minstrel entertainment have said to that? The fact is that Haweis knew all the time that the Christy Minstrels were a sham. He said so. "The manufacture of national music carried on by sham niggers in England is as much like the original article as a penny woodcut is like a line engraving", but he could condone the errors of those with good intentions (and ignore the fact that profit was the motive): "The entertainment is popular, and yet bears some impress of its peculiar and romantic origin. The scent of the roses may be said to hang about it still. We cherish no malignant feeling towards those amiable gentlemen at St. James's Hall, whose ingenious fancy has painted them so much blacker than they really are."

Strangely enough, this sentimentality had its roots in human sympathy and a conception of spiritual values, that came to a climax in religious thought and merged at the end of the century with a rather boastful imperialism. The real strength of the romantic movement was exerted in its earlier years. The description of Vauxhall Gardens in *Sketches by Boz* is the result of keen observation and straight comment, but turn to the epilogue of *Martin Chuzzlewit*—written only about ten years later— and see what Dickens could pour out in a nostalgic mood:

"Thou glidest now into a graver air, an air devoted to old

friends and bygone times; and in thy lingering touch upon the keys, and the rich swelling of the mellow harmony, they rise before thee. The spirit of that old man dead, who delighted to anticipate thy wants, and never ceased to honour thee, is there among the rest, repeating, with a face composed and calm, the words he said to thee upon his bed, and blessing thee!"

The balm of music is used to soothe the mind while Dickens recalls in a dream the past emotions of his reader. The rhythm sways, the images pass before a lulled mind, and the language, archaic, makes a contemporary scene remote. So nauseating to us, yet how the Victorians loved it!

If this were the whole story of romanticism in England there would be little to interest present-day readers. The names of the great singers of those days, however, are still something to wonder at, for mechanical reproduction of sound had not been discovered in time to preserve any records of most of them, and the few whose voices have been recorded by the early twentieth-century apparatus have been unfortunate by reason of the imperfections of the system used. The magic of Jenny Lind and Adelina Patti, and a host of other great singers, must remain a legend, available only in writings that sound so different from those voices. The same is true of the great instrumentalists. Composers are more fortunate, for their scores remain, and even traditions of interpretation. Literature can do so little to reveal the nature of music; all it can do is describe people's reactions to it; yet in this there is so much of interest. Every writer does it in his own way, weaving into his musical recollections his own ideas. Nathaniel Hawthorne listened to the sons of Robert Burns singing their father's verses to the old ballad tunes, and mixed his impression with his own New England republicanism; Thomas Cooper the Chartist thanked God there would be music in heaven; Charles Reade wrote about old violins instructively, and lost himself in human sympathy when he considered the poverty which oppressed a practical musician. Then there are the little glimpses of contemporary life—Thomas Hardy's picture of the passing of the old village choir in *Under the Greenwood Tree*, and Mrs. Gaskell's description of the uncouth manners of the West Riding villagers, contrasted with their love of choral music—especially Handel.

The music of Handel was revered out of all proportion to its merit in the nineteenth century. This is not to say that their favourite *Messiah* has not great merit, but no single composer can be so far above all others as to justify the Victorian elevation of Handel. Even those who were critical of their own age could lose their judgment in contemplation of Handel. In an age when mechanical progress was ever of public interest, Samuel Butler, with a gentle allegory and satire worthy of an earlier age, could find the chinks in the armour of Victorian belief; but he put Handel on a column that lifted him and his music as high above the heads of his readers as Nelson's statue elevates that hero above the others in Trafalgar Square. He wrote little thoughts on Handel and Shakespeare, or Handel and Beethoven, or could see in the shape of the Wetterhorn the outline of the melody in *Messiah* set to the words *And the government shall be upon His shoulders*, and wonder which way Handel went from Germany into Italy. Then there is Butler's fantastic dream-picture of a Handel Festival, with the music rolling down, but all the figures on the stage still, crowned by the organ at their apex; and two little lords come, and discover that the organ keyboard is really a slot into which they can drop a coin, whereupon all the figures on the stage come to life, and start to kill each other. There is small literary merit in these foibles, but the fantasy of the great organ of the mountains with the howling statues, in *Erewhon*, is impressive English, even though it be bad Handelian appreciation.

One should not, perhaps, expect too much from a rebel. Thomas Carlyle strides across the Victorian stage like Wagner's Wotan; not like a Siegfried with a future. Who were the Siegfrieds of Victorian England? Not the artists, not the soldiers, not even the politicians, fulminate as they may, but the scientists.

Charles Darwin and his followers were the spearhead of Victorian unbelief and nineteenth century revolt, yet were they not really in a way the most conservative of all? Was not Darwin a true successor to the eighteenth century Age of Reason? He certainly strove to avoid scientific speculation; to ground his theory firmly on observed facts; yet when he comes to consider music he is the most speculative of them all. He could make a shot at the influence of *tessitura* on musical expression and subjective emotion, but as soon as his theory needs musical understanding it stops for want of elementary knowledge. "Whether the principle of antithesis has come into play with sounds, as might perhaps have been expected, is doubtful." Is it? How is musical form to be considered if we eliminate antithesis? How is tone-colour to be known if not by antithesis? In all human thought there is some spot that the light of reason cannot reach, perhaps through simple ignorance of a fact, perhaps from a flaw in the character. Scientists are not without their flaws, nor have any of them universal knowledge. The subjective interpretation of natural behaviour was as much in evidence in the work of scientists as it was in that of artists. Try as they may, they could not avoid it, and indeed, so long as living things were under consideration, subjective processes were part of the problem to be studied. Some musicians advocated the expression of emotion above everything else, and they were among the greatest minds of the century. The revolt from eighteenth century formalism reached its climax in the music-dramas of Wagner and the symphonic poems of Liszt, Tschaikovsky, and Richard Strauss. German romanticism was predominent in the Englishman's idea of great music. Unquestionably this music was great, but it was not to be what its advocates represented—the music of the future. However, they can hardly be blamed for a prophecy that reflected only a wish, since wishing has so much to do with all prophecy. Men looked back to the bad old days of the 'thirties and 'forties, and gained confidence from the progress that had been made. Queen Victoria drove in her carriage through the streets of London at her two great Jubilees of 1887 and 1897, surrounded by a loving people, the route resplendent with the flags of an empire on which the sun never set, and concert halls resounded to the strains of *The Banner of St. George* and the *Imperial March* of Edward Elgar. Greatness was a British privilege.

Yet the 'nineties saw an artistic rebellion in England, short-lived, it appeared, but effective in a way not obvious at the time. German thought had influenced British music and was even a leaven in British politics. Teutonic opinion stood high in England among the middle classes, and German Universities claimed a growing percentage of the sons of wealthy British merchants and industrialists. France was a good place to visit, and one learned French in a way at all good English schools, but France was nevertheless a place for charm and light amusement rather than for the serious business of culture. In our more pompous moments we were known to use the word "decadent" to describe ideas coming from French writers and painters.

We applied the word with equal confidence to those young artists and writers in our own country who allowed themselves to be influenced by French ideas. The 'nineties saw the beginning and end of one of the most advanced periodicals ever issued in our language—*The Yellow Book*. It struck fresh blows in the eternal aesthetic struggle, for the supporters of this paper were rebels against the smuggery of their time. They played in words with epigrams, and in paint with colour values; the stuff of art they contrasted with the stuff of human emotions. Their dreams were still nostalgic—though they would strenuously have denied this—but they sought an ideal form of society wherein the artist was an aristocrat by artistic right. Oscar Wilde and Aubrey Beardsley dreamed this dream; Beardsley died young and Wilde fell into disgrace; France apparently kept the lead in all that was opposed to German profundity. The public was dubbed stupid and ignorant and should be ignored as far as possible. Writing to Guiraud, Bizet could say: "I dreamed last night that we were all at Naples, installed in a most lovely villa, and living under a government purely artistic. The Senate was made up by Beethoven, Michelangelo, Shakespeare, Giorgione, *e tutti quanti.* The National Guard was no more. In place of it was a huge orchestra of which Litolff was the conductor. All suffrage was denied to idiots, humbugs, schemers, and ignoramuses—that is to say, suffrage was cut down to the smallest proportions imaginable." Passages such as this would attract the attention of readers of *The Yellow Book* in the 'nineties, and though they seemed to fall out of favour for a time, they were to assume importance after the First World War.

The ensuing battle for the establishment of strikingly original types of music is one of the most fascinating in the history of the art, though to many people it seems yet too close to be seen in its true proportions. There are corresponding features, however, in modern literature and painting which help to elucidate the thought of our times, but they are not for this book.

Sir Walter Scott

THE COVENANTERS' STAND

THE LEADING files of the regiment had nearly attained the brow of the hill we have mentioned, when two or three horsemen, speedily discovered to be a part of their own advanced guard, who had acted as a patrol, appeared returning at full gallop, their horses much blown, and the men apparently in a disordered flight. They were followed upon the spur by five or six riders, well armed with sword and pistol, who halted upon the top of the hill, on observing the approach of the Life-Guards. One or two who had carbines dismounted, and, taking a leisurely and deliberate aim at the foremost rank of the regiment, discharged their pieces, by which two troopers were wounded, one severely. They then mounted their horses, and disappeared over the ridge of the hill, retreating with so much coolness as evidently showed, that, on the one hand, they were undismayed at the approach of so considerable a force as was moving against them, and conscious, on the other, that they were supported by numbers sufficient for their protection. This incident occasioned a halt through the whole body of cavalry; and while Claverhouse himself received the report of his advanced guard, which had been thus driven back upon the main body, Lord Evandale advanced to the top of the ridge over which the enemy's horsemen had retired, and Major Allan, Cornet Grahame, and the other officers, employed themselves in extricating the regiment from the broken ground, and drawing them up on the side of the hill in two lines, the one to support the other.

The word was then given to advance; and in a few minutes the first lines stood on the brow and commanded the prospect on the other side. The second line closed upon them, and also the rear-guard with the prisoners; so that Morton and his companions in captivity could, in like manner, see the form of opposition which was now offered to the farther progress of their captors.

The brow of the hill, on which the royal Life-Guards were now drawn up, sloped downwards (on the side opposite to that which they had ascended) with a gentle declivity, for more than a quarter of a mile, and presented ground, which, though unequal in some places, was not altogether unfavourable for the manœuvres of cavalry, until near the bottom, where the slope terminated in a marshy level, traversed through its whole length by what seemed either a natural gully, or a deep artificial drain, the sides of which were broken by springs, trenches filled with water, out of which peats and turf had been dug, and here and there by some straggling thickets of alders that loved the moistness so well, that they continued to live as bushes, although too much dwarfed by the sour soil and the stagnant bog-water to ascend into trees. Beyond this ditch, or gully, the ground rose to a second heathy swell, or rather hill, near to the foot of which, and as if with the object of defending the broken ground and ditch that covered their front, the body of insurgents appeared to be drawn up with the purpose of abiding battle.

Their infantry was divided into three lines. The first, tolerably provided with fire-arms, were advanced almost close to the verge of the bog, so that their fire must necessarily annoy the royal cavalry as they descended the opposite hill, the whole front of which was exposed, and would probably be yet more fatal if they attempted to cross the morass. Behind this first line was a body of pikemen, designed for their support in case the dragoons should force the passage of the marsh. In their rear was their third line, consisting of countrymen armed with scythes set straight on poles, hayforks, spits, clubs, goads, fish-spears, and such other rustic implements as hasty resentment had converted into instruments of war. On each flank of the infantry, but a little backward from the bog, as if to allow themselves dry and solid ground whereon to act in case their enemies should force the pass, there was drawn up a small body of cavalry, who were, in general, but indifferently armed, and worse mounted, but full of zeal for the cause, being chiefly either landholders of small property, or farmers of the better class, whose means enabled them to serve on horseback. A few of those who had been engaged in driving back the advanced guard of the royalists, might now be seen returning slowly towards their own squadrons. These were the only individuals of the insurgent army which seemed to be in motion. All the others stood firm and motionless, as the grey stones that lay scattered on the heath around them.

The total number of the insurgents might amount to about a thousand men; but of these there were scarce a hundred cavalry nor were the half of them even tolerably armed. The strength of their position, however, and the sense of their having taken a desperate step, the superiority of their numbers, but, above all, the ardour of their enthusiasm, were the means on which their leaders reckoned, for supplying the want of arms, equipage, and military discipline.

On the side of the hill that rose above the array of battle which they had adopted, were seen the women and even the children, whom zeal, opposed to persecution, had driven into the wilderness.

They seemed stationed there to be spectators of the engagement, by which their own fate, as well as that of their parents, husbands, and sons, was to be decided. Like the females of the ancient German tribes, the shrill cries which they raised, when they beheld the glittering ranks of their enemy appear on the brow of the opposing eminence, acted as an incentive to their relatives to fight to the last in defence of that which was dearest to them. Such exhortations seemed to have their full and emphatic effect: for a wild halloo, which went from rank to rank on the appearance of the soldiers, intimated the resolution of the insurgents to fight to the uttermost.

As the horsemen halted their lines on the ridge of the hill, their trumpets and kettle-drums sounded a bold and warlike flourish of menace and defiance, that rang along the waste like the shrill summons of a destroying angel. The wanderers, in answer, united their voices, and sent forth, in solemn modulation, the two first verses of the seventy-sixth Psalm, according to the metrical version of the Scottish Kirk:

> "In Judah's land God is well known,
> His name's in Israel great:
> In Salem is his tabernacle,
> In Zion is his seat.

> "There arrows of the bow he brake,
> The shield, the sword, the war.
> More glorious thou than hills of prey,
> More excellent art far."

A shout, or rather a solemn acclamation, attended the close of the stanza; and after a dead pause, the second verse was resumed by the insurgents, who applied the destruction of the Assyrians as prophetic of the issue of their own impending contest:

> "Those that were stout of heart are spoil'd,
> They slept their sleep outright;

And none of those their hands did find,
That were the men of might.

"When thy rebuke, O Jacob's God,
Had forth against them past,
Their horses and their chariots both
Were in a deep sleep cast."

There was another acclamation, which was followed by the most profound silence.

While these solemn sounds, accented by a thousand voices, were prolonged against the waste hills, Claverhouse looked with great attention on the ground, and on the order of battle which the wanderers had adopted, and in which they determined to await the assault.

"The churls", he said, "must have some old soldiers with them; it is no rustic that made choice of that ground."

"Burley is said to be with them for certain", answered Lord Evandale, "and also Hackston of Rathillet, Paton of Meadowhead, Cleland, and some other men of military skill."

"I judged as much", said Claverhouse, "from the style in which these detached horsemen leapt their horses over the ditch, as they returned to their position. It was easy to see that there were a few roundheaded troopers amongst them, the true spawn of the old Covenant. We must manage this matter warily as well as boldly. Evandale, let the officers come to this knoll."

He moved to a small moss-grown cairn, probably the resting-place of some Celtic chief of other times, and the call of "Officers to the front", soon brought them around their commander.

"I do not call you around me, gentlemen", said Claverhouse, "in the formal capacity of a council of war, for I will never turn over to others the responsibility which my rank imposes on myself. I only want the benefit of your opinions, reserving to myself, as most men do when they ask advice, the liberty of following my own.—What say you, Cornet Grahame?

Shall we attack those fellows who are bellowing yonder? You are youngest and hottest, and therefore will speak first whether I will or no."

"Then", said Cornet Grahame, "while I have the honour to carry the standard of the Life-Guards, it shall never, with my will, retreat before rebels. I say, charge, in God's name and the King's!"

"And what say you, Allan?" continued Claverhouse, "for Evandale is so modest, we shall never get him to speak till you have said what you have to say."

"These fellows", said Major Allan, an old cavalier officer of experience, "are three or four to one—I should not mind that much upon a fair field, but they are posted in a very formidable strength, and show no inclination to quit it. I therefore think, with deference to Cornet Grahame's opinion, that we should draw back to Tillietudlem, occupy the pass between the hills and the open country, and send for reinforcements to my Lord Ross, who is lying at Glasgow with a regiment of infantry. In this way we should cut them off from the Strath of Clyde, and either compel them to come out of their stronghold, and give us battle on fair terms, or, if they remain here, we will attack them as soon as our infantry has joined us, and enabled us to act with effect among these ditches, bogs, and quagmires."

"Pshaw!" said the young Cornet, "what signifies strong ground, when it is only held by a crew of canting, psalm-singing old women?"

"A man may fight never the worse", retorted Major Allan, "for honouring both his Bible and Psalter. These fellows will prove as stubborn as steel; I know them of old."

"Their nasal psalmody", said the Cornet, "reminds our Major of the race of Dunbar."

"Had you been at that race, young man", retorted Allan, "you would have wanted nothing to remind you of it for the longest day you have to live."

Old Mortality, Ch. XV.

Charles Lamb

A CHAPTER ON EARS

I HAVE no ear——

Mistake me not, reader—nor imagine that I am by nature destitute of those exterior twin appendages, hanging ornaments, and (architecturally speaking) handsome volutes to the human capital. Better my mother had never borne me.—I am, I think, rather delicately than copiously provided with those conduits; and I feel no disposition to envy the mule for his plenty, or the mole for her exactness, in those ingenious labyrinthine inlets—those indispensable side-intelligencers.

Neither have I incurred, or done anything to incur, with Defoe, that hideous disfigurement, which constrained him to draw upon assurance—to feel "quite unabashed", and at ease upon that article. I was never, I thank my stars, in the pillory; nor, if I read them aright, is it within the compass of my destiny, that I ever should be.

When therefore I say that I have no ear, you will understand me to mean—*for music*. To say that this heart never melted at the concord of sweet sounds, would be a foul self-libel. "*Water parted from the sea*" never fails to move it strangely. So does "*In Infancy*", but they were used to be sung at her harpsichord (the old-fashioned instrument in vogue in those days) by a gentlewoman—the gentlest, sure, that ever merited the appellation—the sweetest—why should I hesitate to name Mrs. S—, once the blooming Fanny Weatheral of the Temple—who had power to thrill the soul of Elia, small imp as he was, even in his long coats; and to make him glow, tremble, and blush with a passion, that not faintly indicated the day-spring of that absorbing sentiment which was afterwards destined to overwhelm and subdue his nature quite for Alice W—n.

I even think that *sentimentally* I am disposed to harmony. But *organically* I am incapable of a tune. I have been practising "*God Save the King*" all my life; whistling and humming it over to myself in solitary corners; and am not yet arrived, they tell me, within many quavers of it. Yet hath the loyalty of Elia never been impeached.

I am not without suspicion, that I have an undeveloped faculty of music within me. For thrumming, in my wild way, on my friend A.'s piano, the other morning, while he was engaged in an adjoining parlour,—on his return he was pleased to say, *"he thought it could not be the maid!"* On his first surprise at hearing the keys touched in somewhat an airy and masterful way, not dreaming of me, his suspicions had lighted on *Jenny*. But a grace, snatched from a superior refinement, soon convinced him that some being—technically perhaps deficient, but higher informed from a principle common to all the fine arts—had swayed the keys to a mood which Jenny, with all her (less cultivated) enthusiasm, could never have elicited from them. I mention this as a proof of my friend's penetration, and not with any view of disparaging Jenny.

Scientifically I could never be made to understand (yet have I taken some pains) what a note of music is; or how one note should differ from another. Much less in voices can I distinguish a soprano from a tenor. Only sometimes the thorough-bass I contrive to guess at, from its being supereminently harsh and disagreeable. I tremble, however, for my misapplication of the simplest terms of *that* which I disclaim. While I profess my ignorance, I scarce know what to *say* I am ignorant of. I hate, perhaps, by misnomers. *Sostenuto* and *Adagio* stand in the like relation of obscurity to me; and *Sol, Fa, Mi, Re,* is as conjuring as *Baralipton*.

It is hard to stand alone in an age like this,—(constituted to the quick and critical perception of all harmonious combinations, I verily believe, beyond all preceding ages, since Jubal stumbled upon the gamut), to remain, as it were, singly unimpressible to the magic influences of an art, which is said to have such an especial stroke as soothing, elevating, and refining the passions.— Yet, rather than break the candid current of my confessions, I must avow to you that I have received a great deal more pain than pleasure from this so cried-up faculty.

I am constitutionally susceptible of noises. A carpenter's hammer, in a warm summer noon, will fret me into more than midsummer madness. But those unconnected, unset sounds, are nothing to the measured malice of music. The ear is passive to those single strokes; willingly enduring stripes while it hath no task to con. To music it cannot be passive. It will strive— mine at least will—spite of its inaptitude, to thrid the maze; like an unskilled eye painfully poring upon hieroglyphics. I have sat through an Italian Opera, till, for sheer pain, and inexplicable anguish, I have rushed out into the noisiest places of the crowded streets, to solace myself with sounds, which I was not obliged to follow, and get rid of the distracting torment of endless, fruitless, barren attention! I take refuge in the unpretending assemblage of honest common-life sounds;—and the purgatory of the Enraged Musician becomes my paradise.

I have sat at an Oratorio (that profanation of the purposes of the cheerful playhouse) watching the faces of the auditory in the pit (what a contrast to Hogarth's Laughing Audience!) immovable, or affecting some faint emotion—till (as some have said, that our occupations in the next world will be but a shadow of what delighted us in this) I have imagined myself in the same cold Theatre in Hades, where some of the *forms* of the earthly one should be kept up, with none of the *enjoyment*; or like that

—PARTY IN A PARLOUR
ALL SILENT, AND ALL DAMNED.

Above all, those insufferable concertos, and pieces of music, as they are called, do plague and embitter my apprehension.— Words are something; but to be exposed to an endless battery of mere sounds; to be long a dying; to lie stretched upon a rack of roses; to keep up languor by unintermitted effort; to pile honey upon sugar, and sugar upon honey, to an interminable tedious sweetness; to fill up sound with feeling, and strain ideas to keep pace with it; to gaze on empty frames, and be forced to make the pictures for yourself; to read a book, *all stops*, and be obliged to supply the verbal matter; to invent extempore tragedies to answer to the vague gestures of an inexplicable rambling mime—these are faint shadows of what I have undergone from a series of the ablest-executed pieces of this empty *instrumental music.*

I deny not, that in the opening of a concert, I have experienced something vastly lulling and agreeable:—afterwards followeth the languor and oppression.—Like that disappointing book in Patmos; or, like the comings on of melancholy, described by Burton, doth music make her first insinuating approaches:— "Most pleasant it is to such as are melancholy given, to walk alone in some solitary grove, betwixt wood and water, by some brook side, and to meditate upon some delightsome and pleasant subject, which shall affect him most, *amabis insania,* and *mentis gratissimus error.* A most incomparable delight to build castles in the air, to go smiling to ourselves, acting an infinite variety of parts, which they suppose, and strongly imagine, they act, or that they see done.—So delightsome these toys at first, they could spend whole days and nights without sleep, even whole years in such contemplations, and fantastical meditations, which are like so many dreams, and will hardly be drawn from them—winding and unwinding themselves as so many clocks, and still pleasing their humours, until at last the SCENE TURNS UPON A SUDDEN. and they being now habituated to such meditations and solitary places, can endure no company, can think of nothing but harsh and distasteful subjects. Fear, sorrow, suspicion, *subrusticus pudor,* discontent, cares, and weariness of life, surprise them on a sudden, and they can think of nothing else: continually suspecting, no sooner are their eyes open, but this infernal plague of melancholy seizeth on them, and terrifies their souls, representing some dismal object to their minds; which now, by no means, no labour, no persuasions, they can avoid, they cannot be rid of, they cannot resist."

Something like this "SCENE TURNING" I have experienced at the evening parties, at the house of my good Catholic friend *Nov*—; who, by the aid of a capital organ, himself the most finished of players, converts his drawing-room into a chapel, his week days into Sundays, and these latter into minor heavens.[1]

When my friend commences upon one of those solemn anthems, which peradventure struck upon my heedless ear, rambling in the side aisles of the dim Abbey, some five-and-thirty years since, waking a new sense, and putting a soul of old religion into my young apprehension—(whether it be *that*, in which the Psalmist, weary of the persecutions of bad men, wisheth to himself dove's wings—or *that other* which, with a like measure of sobriety and pathos, inquireth by what means the young man shall cleanse his mind)—a holy calm pervadeth me.—I am for the time

> —rapt above earth,
> And possess joys not promised at my birth.

But when this master of the spell, not content to have laid a soul prostrate, goes on, in his power, to inflict more bliss than lies in her capacity to receive—impatient to overcome her "earthly" with this "heavenly",—still pouring in, for protracted hours, fresh waves and fresh from the sea of sound, or from that exhausted *German* ocean, above which, in triumphant progress, dolphin-seated, ride those Arions *Haydn*, and *Mozart*, with their attendant Tritons, *Bach*, *Beethoven*, and a countless tribe, whom to attempt to reckon up would plunge me again in the deeps,—I stagger under the weight of harmony, reeling to and fro at my wits' end;—clouds, as of frankincense, oppress me—priests, altars, censers, dazzle before me—the genius of *his* religion hath me in her toils—a shadowy triple tiara invests the brow of my friend, late so naked, so ingenuous—he is Pope,—and by him sits, like as in the anomaly of dreams, a she-Pope, too,—tricoronated like himself!—I am converted, and yet a Protestant;—at once *malleus hereticorum*, and myself grand heresiarch: or three heresies centre in my person:—I am Marcion, Elbion, and Cerinthus—Gog and Magog—what not?—till the coming in of the

[1] I have been there, and still would go;
'Tis like a little heaven below.—Dr. Watts.

friendly supper-tray dissipates the figment, and a draught of true Lutheran beer (in which chiefly my friend shows himself no bigot) at once reconciles me to the rationalities of a purer faith; and restores to me the genuine unterrifying aspects of my pleasant-countenanced host and hostess.

The Essays of Elia

William Hazlitt

THE ITALIAN OPERA IN LONDON

IN SCHLEGEL'S work on the Drama, there are the following remarks on the nature of the Opera:

"In Tragedy the chief object is the poetry, and every other thing is subordinate to it; but in the Opera, the poetry is merely an accessory, the means of connecting the different parts together, and it is almost buried under its associates. The best prescription for the composition of the text of an Opera is to give a poetical sketch, which may be afterwards filled up and coloured by the other arts. This anarchy of the arts, where music, dancing, and decoration endeavour to surpass each other by the profuse display of dazzling charms, constitutes the very essence of the Opera. What sort of opera music would it be, where the words should receive a mere rhythmical accompaniment of the simplest modulations? The fantastic magic of the Opera consists altogether in the luxurious competition of the different means, and in the perplexity of an overflowing superfluity. This would at once be destroyed by an approximation to the severity of the ancient taste in any one point, even in that of costume; for the contrast would render the variety in all the other departments quite insupportable. The costume of the Opera ought to be dazzling, and overladen with ornaments; and hence many things which have been censured as unnatural, such as exhibiting heroes warbling and trilling in the excess of despondency, are perfectly justifiable. This fairy world is not peopled by real men, but by a singular kind of singing creatures. Neither is it any disadvantage to us, that the Opera is conveyed in a language which is not generally understood; the text is altogether lost in the music, and the language, the most harmonious and musical, and which contains the greatest number of open vowels and distinct accents for recitative, is therefore the best."

The foregoing remarks give the best account we have seen of that splendid exhibition, the Italian Opera. These German critics can explain every thing, and upon any given occasion, *make the worse appear the better reason.* Their theories are always at variance with common sense, and we shall not in the present instance, undertake to decide between them. There is one thing, however, which we will venture to decide, which is, that the feelings of the English people must undergo some very elaborate process (metaphysical or practical) before they are thoroughly reconciled to this union of different elements, the consistency and harmony of which depends on their contradiction and discord. We take it, the English are so far from being an opera-going, that they are not even a play-going people, from constitution. You can hardly get them to speak their sentiments, much less to sing them, or to hear them sung with any real sympathy. The boxes, splendid as they are, and splendid as the appearance of those in them is, do not breathe a spirit of enjoyment. They are rather like the sick wards of luxury and idleness, where the people of a certain class are condemned to perform the quarantine of fashion for the evening. The rest of the spectators are sulky and self-important, and the only idea which each person has in his head, seems to be that he is at the opera. Little interest is shown in the singing or dancing, little pleasure appears to be derived from either, and the audience seem only to be stunned and stupified with wonder. The satisfaction which the English feel in this entertainment is very much *against the grain.* They are a people, jealous of being pleased in any way but their own.

We were particularly struck with the force of these remarks the other evening in the gallery, where our fellow-countrymen seemed to be only upon their good behaviour or self-defence against the ill-behaviour of others, some persons asserting their right of talking loud about their own affairs, and others resenting this, not as an interruption of their pleasures, but as an encroachment on their privileges. Soon after a Frenchman came in, and his eye at once fastened upon the ballet. At a particular air, he could no longer contain himself, but joined in chorus in an agreeable under-voice, as if he expected others to keep time to him, and exclaiming, while he wiped his forehead from an exuberance of satisfaction, his eyes glistened, and his face shining, *"Ah c'est charmant, c'est charmant!"* Now this, being ourselves English, we confess, gave us more pleasure than the opera or the ballet, in both of which, however, we felt a considerable degree of melancholy satisfaction, *selon la coutume de notre pays—* according to the custom of our country.

The opera was *Cosi fan Tutte*, with Mozart's music, and the ballet was the *Dansomanie*. The music of the first of these is really enough (to borrow a phrase from a person who was also a great man in his way) "to draw three souls out of one weaver:" and as to the ballet, it might make a Frenchman forget his country and all other things. This ballet is certainly the essence of a ballet. What a grace and liveliness there is in it! What spirit and invention! What can exceed the ingenuity of the dance in which the favoured lover joins in with his mistress and the rival, and makes all sorts of advances to her, and receives her favours, her pressures of the hand, and even kisses, without being found out by the other, who thinks all these demonstrations of fondness intended for him! What an enthusiasm for art in the character of the master of the house, who is seized by the *Dansomanie*! What a noble and disinterested zeal in the pursuit and encouragement of his favourite science! What a mechanical spriteliness in all about him, particularly in the servant who throws down a whole equipage of china, while he is dancing with it on his head, and is rewarded by his master for this proof of devotion to his interests! What a sympathy throughout between the heels and the head, between the heart and the fingers' ends! The *Minuet de la Cour*, danced in full dresses, and with the well-known accompaniment of the music, put us in mind of the old chivalrous times of the Duke de Nemours and the Princess of Cleves, or of what really seems to us longer ago, the time when we ourselves used to be called out of school before the assembled taste and fashion of the neighbourhood, to go through this very dance with the partner whom we had selected for the purpose, and presented with a bunch of flowers on the occasion!

The Opera had less justice done it than the Ballet. The laughing Trio was spoiled by Mr. Naldi, who performs the part of an "Old Philosopher" in it, but who is more like an impudent valet or *major-domo* of an hotel. We never saw any one so much at home; who seems so little conscious of the existence of any one but himself, and who throws his voice, his arms and legs about with such a total disregard of *bienseance*. The character is a kind of Opera Pandarus, who exposes the inconstancy of two young ladies, by entangling them in an intrigue with their own lovers in disguise. Mr. Braham, we are told, sings Mozart with a peculiar greatness of gusto. But this greatness of gusto does not appear to us the real excellence of Mozart. The song beginning *Secondate*, in which he and his friend (Signor Begri) call upon the gentle zephyrs by moonlight to favour their design, is exquisite, and "floats upon the air, smoothing the raven down of darkness till it smiles."

"And Silence wish'd, she might be nevermore
Still to be so displaced."

Madame Fodor's voice does not harmonize with the music of this composer. It is hard, metallic, and jars like the reverberation of a tight string. Mozart's music should seem to come from the air, and return to it. Madame Vestris is a pretty little figure, and is in this respect a contrast to Madame Fordor.

The Examiner, 1816

William Gardiner

THE HIGHEST DEGREE OF PERFECTION

THE FORMATION of the musical ear depends on early impressions. Infants who are placed within the constant hearing of musical sounds, soon learn to appreciate them, and nurses have the merit of giving the first lessons in melody; for we learn from the lives of eminent composers, that their early fondness for the art may be traced to the ditties of the nursery.

Children brought up in musical families, often entertained by the sound of musical instruments, so soon acquire a musical sense as, in some instances, to be regarded as prodigies. Mozart began to compose at the age of four; and in a paper read before the Royal Society by Doctor Burney, it is affirmed that Crotch played the air of *"Let ambition fire thy mind"* when only two years old.

By practice, the discriminating powers of the ear may be carried to the highest degree of perfection. The success of thieves and gamblers depends upon its quickness. Since the money has been recoined, the regularity with which each piece is struck gives them a uniformity of sound that is very remarkable. ... Bankers quickly discover the least deviation from the proper tone, by which they readily detect the counterfeits. In the tossing up of money, gamblers can perceive a difference in the sound, whether it falls upon one side or the other. Pye-men are furnished with a covering to their baskets made of a smooth plate of metal, by which they take in the unwary, as they readily tell which side is uppermost by the sound upon the plate, though concealed by the hand.

The atmosphere is the grand medium by which sound is conveyed, though recent discoveries prove that other bodies conduct it with greater expedition, as in the instance of vibrating a tuning fork, to the stem of which is attached a packthread string; on the other end being wrapt round the little finger, and placed in the chamber of the ear, the sound will be audibly conveyed to the distance of two hundred yards, though not perceptible to any bystander. Miners, in boring for coal, can tell by the sound what substance they are penetrating; and a recent discovery is that of applying a listening-tube to the breast to detect the motions of the heart. The quickness which some persons possess in distinguishing the smaller sounds, is very remarkable. A friend of the writer has declared he could readily perceive the motion of a flea, when on his nightcap, by the sound emitted by the machinery of his leaping powers. However extraordinary this may appear, we find a similar statement is given in the ingenious work upon insects, by Kirby and Spence, who say, "I *know* of no other insect, the tread of which is accompanied by sound, except the flea, whose steps a lady assured me she always hears when it passes over her nightcap, and that it clacks as if it was walking in pattens!" If we can suppose the ear to be alive to such delicate vibrations, certainly there is nothing in the way of sound too difficult for it to achieve. To accustom ourselves to listen with attention, is the first step to improvement.

By pursuing a course of study in harmony, we soon acquire what is termed a musical ear, and ultimately find no difficulty in determining the finest gradations. From what has been said, it must be obvious, that the improvement of the ear depends solely upon the attention with which it is used and exerted, as has been shown in the instances of blind people. That there is a knack in listening, no one can doubt, as we frequently find persons, who sing and play out of tune, readily distinguish this defect in others, but have not the habit of detecting this same fault in themselves. The power we have of recollecting sounds, or calling up former impressions, is much greater in some persons than in others; but most persons have experienced, that when they have been delighted with a new air, without any effort of their own, how it will haunt them for days.

The faculties of the ear, then, are by no means fully developed.

Every new author in musical composition offers some new stimulus to the auditory sense. The sober strains of the last age would be considered intolerably dull and stupid by the listening public of the present day. Even the fine compositions of Mozart are beginning to be thought heavy when compared with the brilliant strains of Rossini. The true composer may be said to *"live, move, and have his being"* in the midst of sounds. To him they are the materials of his art. Not so with the painter; he loves stillness and repose, and rambles in search of quiet spots. Hogarth rather painted his *own* feelings in his picture of the enraged musician, than those of a composer.

It has been remarked, that poets become blind, and musicians deaf. Homer, Milton, and Delisle—with Gretry and Beethoven, are instances. Then may we not suppose, that the decay of the organ arises from the internal action of the mind, calling up ideas of light and sound?

The Music of Nature, 1832

Thomas Cooper

AN ABSORBING PASSION

BUT A new attraction arose at last; and all resolves about study, and purposes of intellectual progress, and interests however important, were sacrificed for my new passion. A few young men wished to form a Choral Society, and asked me to allow them the use of my school-room for rehearsals. I consented readily, and became a member of the new society—taking my stand, weekly, as a tenor singer in the choruses. My heart and brain were soon on flame with the worship of Handel's grandeur, and with the love of his sweetness and tenderness. They made me their secretary; and my head went to work to make the music of the Choral Society worth hearing in old cathedralled Lincoln.

I planned, I visited, I wooed, I entreated, till I obtained the aid and co-operation of the best musicians and the best singers in

the ancient city. Like every true reformer, I had to put down
the authority of the imperfect, and put the authoritative perfect
in its place. Over the company of raw amateurs—despite some
grumbling—I succeeded in placing the most perfect "singer at
sight", and most thoroughly experienced person in the music
of Handel, to be found in the whole city, as conductor; the best
violinist in the city, as leader; the best alto and tenor singers
in the city, as leaders of their parts in the choruses, and as principal
solo singers; the organist of the cathedral, as leader on the viola;
the best violoncello player in Lincoln, as leader on his instrument;
while I also secured the aid of an experienced trumpeter. We
already had the aid of a good double-bass player, who was also
a sound timist. And I may also say that I had most valuable
aid, by way of counsel and advice, from that most accomplished
musician, the late Rev. George S. Dickson, Incumbent of St.
Swithin's, Lincoln.

The next step was to obtain funds, that professional men
might be remunerated, and the society held together by something more than mere enthusiasm. I wrote to the nobility,
gentry, and clergy of the county and the city, and to all members
of Parliament for Lincolnshire; and was successful in almost
every case. I raised an income of £200 for the society's first
year. Then I besought the Dean, the Precentor, and Sub-dean
to lend their powers of persuasion; and the incumbent of the
most central church in the city granted us the use of it for our
public concerts of sacred music. Mr. Whall, the most thoroughly
competent organist in Lincoln, presided at the organ; and, before
a crowded audience, the transcendent "Messiah", the noble
"Dettingen Te Deum", the brilliant and warlike "Judas
Maccabaeus", the gorgeous "Solomon", the sublime "Israel in
Egypt", and other oratorios of Handel, were performed with an
enthusiasm that had never before been witnessed in Lincoln.
The "Creation" of Haydn, and scattered choral pieces of Mozart
and Beethoven, were also given.

Nor was the solo singing of a mean character. Our conductor,
George Brooke, of the cathedral choir, would have attracted

admiration, as a bass singer of great original powers of expression, and great capability of execution, with the most critical audience in the kingdom. The tenor singing of dear departed Charles Ashton—a universal favourite in Lincoln—was the sweetest I ever heard, except Braham's. Mr. Knowles, our alto solo singer, was not only a very pleasant vocalist, but a competent musician; and is, at the moment I write, a member of the choir in St. George's Chapel, Windsor.

I raised a separate subscription of twenty guineas, for the purchase of concert drums; bought a chromatic slide trumpet at the urgent request of our trumpeter; formed a rich musical library, comprising the forty thick folio volumes of Arnold's complete score of Handel, with German scores of the "Creation", the "Requiem", and the "Mount of Olives"—for the use of the society. I say, *I* did all this—for, although I met a committee of the performers, that conferred together about the selection of choruses and solos for each concert, as it drew nigh, they took no part in the real business of the society. I had all that to plan and execute for myself.

What mad enthusiasm I felt for music! I often sat up the greater part of a night to transact the writing necessary for the furtherance of the prosperity of that Choral Society. I walked, I ran, I jumped, about the city—I climbed its "steep hill" often half a dozen times in a day—to win subscribers and collect subscriptions, and get performers to be punctual at the rehearsals, and to reconcile their petty animosities and keep them united; and I also spent some little money on the darling project of making music successful in Lincoln. I was ever striving to obtain more subscriptions, that our best performers might be better paid—though I would have scorned to take one farthing myself. The enjoyment—the rapture—I had in listening to the music, was more than a reward for whatever time I gave to the society, or interest I sacrificed for it.

But the check to my enthusiasm came; and the end of all this passionate indulgence of the one sense of hearing—did I say? Nay, if there were not *mind* in music, it could not master us in this way, and to the degree that it masters many. A passion for music is something far above the mere indulgence of feeling. Oh, how easily I could again yield to it! But I dare not. Thank God! we shall have music in heaven; and I can wait for it, till I get thither, remembering that the music of heaven will unspeakably transcend all the music of earth.

I say the end came. What no one had thought of trying to do till I did it—and what all acknowledged I had done so well— was deemed, at first, *in whispers*, an assumption of authority, and, at last, and *aloud*, and to my face, a most shameful tyranny! I was opposed,—I was thwarted,—I was "called to account",— I was advised to resign,—I was threatened with dethronement;— and so, eventually, I *abdicated*, and left the Lincoln Choral Society, which had been my idol and my passion, to conduct itself.

The Life of Thomas Cooper (the Chartist)
Written by Himself

Charles Dickens

VAUXHALL GARDENS BY DAY

THERE WAS a time when if a man ventured to wonder how Vauxhall-gardens would look by day, he was hailed with a shout of derision at the absurdity of the idea. Vauxhall by daylight! A porter-pot without porter, the House of Commons without the Speaker, a gas-lamp without the gas—pooh, nonsense, the thing was not to be thought of. It was rumoured, too, in those times, that Vauxhall-gardens by day, were the scene of secret and hidden experiments; that there, carvers were exercised in the mystic art of cutting a moderate-sized ham into slices thin enough to pave the whole of the grounds; that beneath the shade of the tall trees, studious men were constantly engaged in chemical experiments, with the view of discovering how much water a bowl of negus could possibly bear; and that in some retired nooks, appropriated to the study of ornithology, other sage and learned men were, by a process known only to themselves, incessantly employed in reducing fowls to a mere combination of skin and bone.

Vague rumours of this kind, together with many others of a similar nature, cast over Vauxhall-gardens an air of deep mystery; and as there is a great deal in the mysterious, there is no doubt that to a good many people, at all events, the pleasure they afforded was not a little enhanced by this very circumstance.

Of this class of people we confess to having made one. We loved to wander among those illuminated groves, thinking of the patient and laborious researches which had been carried on there during the day, and witnessing their results in the suppers which were served up beneath the light of lamps and to the sound of music at night. The temples and saloons and cosmoramas and fountains glittered and sparkled before our eyes; the beauty of the lady singers and the elegant deportment of the gentlemen, captivated our hearts; a few hundred thousand of additional lamps dazzled our senses; a bowl or two of punch bewildered our brains; and we were happy.

In an evil hour, the proprietors of Vauxhall-gardens took to opening them by day. We regretted this, as rudely and harshly disturbing that veil of mystery which had hung about the property for many years, and which none but the noonday sun, and the late Mr. Simpson, had ever penetrated. We shrunk from going; at this moment we scarcely know why. Perhaps a morbid consciousness of approaching disappointment —perhaps a fatal presentiment—perhaps the weather; whatever it was, we did *not* go until the second or third announcement of a race between two balloons tempted us, and we went.

We paid our shilling at the gate, and then we saw for the first time, that the entrance, if there had been any magic about it at all, was now decidely disenchanted, being, in fact, nothing more or less than a combination of very roughpainted boards and sawdust. We glanced at the orchestra and supper-room as we hurried past—we just recognised them, and that was all. We bent our steps to the firework-ground; there, at least, we should not be disappointed. We reached it, and stood rooted to the spot with mortification and astonishment. *That* the Moorish tower—that wooden shed with a door in the centre, and daubs of crimson and yellow all round, like a gigantic watchcase! *That* the place where night after night we had beheld the undaunted Mr. Blackmore make his terrific ascent, surrounded by flames of fire, and peals of artillery, and where the white garments of Madame Somebody (we forget even her name now), who nobly devoted her life to the manufacture of fireworks, had so often been seen fluttering in the wind, as she called up a red, blue, or party-coloured light to illumine her temple! *That* the—but at this moment the bell rung; the people scampered away, pell-mell, to the spot from whence the sound proceeded; and we, from the mere force of habit, found ourself running among the first, as if for very life.

It was for the concert in the orchestra. A small party of dismal men in cocked hats were "executing" the overture to *Tancredi*, and a numerous assemblage of ladies and gentlemen, with their families, had rushed from their half-emptied stout mugs in the supper boxes, and crowded to the spot. Intense was the low murmur of admiration when a particularly small gentleman, in a dress coat, led on a particularly tall lady in a blue sarcenet pelisse and bonnet of the same, ornamented with large white feathers, and forthwith commenced a plaintive duet.

We knew the small gentleman well; we had seen a lithographed semblance of him, on many a piece of music, with his mouth wide open as if in the act of singing; a wine-glass in his hand; and a table with two decanters and four pine-apples on it in the background. The tall lady, too, we had gazed on, lost in raptures of admiration, many and many a time—how different people *do* look by daylight, and without punch, to be sure! It was a beautiful duet: first the small gentleman asked a question, and then the tall lady answered it; then the small gentleman and the tall lady sang together most melodiously; then the small gentleman went through a little piece of vehemence by himself, and got very tenor indeed, in the excitement of his feelings, to which the tall lady responded in a similar manner; then the small gentleman had a shake or two, after which the tall lady had the same, and then they both merged imperceptibly into the original air: and the band wound themselves up to a pitch of fury, and the small gentleman handed the tall lady out, and the applause was rapturous.

The comic singer, however, was the especial favourite; we really thought that a gentleman, with his dinner in his pocket-handkerchief, who stood near us, would have fainted with excess of joy. A marvellously facetious gentleman that comic singer is; his distinguishing characteristics are, a wig approaching to the flaxen, and an aged countenance, and he bears the name of one of the English counties, if we recollect right. He sang a very good song about the seven ages, the first half-hour of which afforded the assembly the purest delight; of the rest we can make no report, as we did not stay to hear any more.

We walked about, and met with a disappointment at every turn; our favourite views were mere patches of paint; the fountain that had sparkled so showily by lamp-light, presented very much the appearance of a water-pipe that had burst; all the ornaments were dingy, and all the walks gloomy. There was a spectral attempt at rope-dancing in the little open theatre. The sun shone upon the spangled dresses of the performers, and their evolutions were about as inspiriting and appropriate as a country-dance in a family vault. So we retraced our steps to the firework-ground, and mingled with the little crowd of people who were contemplating Mr. Green.

Some half-dozen men were restraining the impetuosity of one of the balloons, which was completely filled, and had the car already attached; and as rumours had gone abroad that a Lord was "going up", the crowd were more than usually anxious and talkative. There was one little man in faded black, with a dirty face and a rusty black neckerchief with a red border, tied in a narrow wisp round his neck, who entered into conversation with everybody, and had something to say upon every remark that was made within his hearing. He was standing with his arms folded, staring up at the balloon, and every now and then vented his feelings of reverence for the aeronaut, by saying, as he looked round to catch somebody's eye, "He's a rum 'un is Green; think o' this here being up'ards of his two hundredth ascent; ecod, the man as is ekal to Green never had the toothache yet, nor won't have within this hundred year, and that's all about it. When you meets with real talent, and native, too, encourage it, that's what I say;" and when he had delivered himself to this effect, he would fold his arms with more determination than ever, and stare at the balloon with a sort of admiring defiance of any other man alive, beyond himself and Green, that impressed the crowd with the opinion that he was an oracle.

"Ah, you're very right, sir", said another gentleman, with his wife, and children, and mother, and wife's sister, and a host of female friends, in all the gentility of white pocket-handkerchiefs, frills, and spencers, "Mr. Green is a steady hand, sir, and there's no fear about him."

"Fear!" said the little man: "isn't it a lovely thing to see him and his wife a going up in one balloon, and his own son and *his* wife a jostling up against them in another, and all of them going twenty or thirty mile in three hours or so, and then coming back in pochayses? I don't know where this here science is to stop, mind you; that's what bothers me."

Here there was considerable talking among the females in the spencers.

"What's the ladies a laughing at, sir?" inquired the little man, condescendingly.

"It's only my sister Mary", said one of the girls, "as says she hopes his lordship won't be frightened when he's in the car, and want to come out again."

"Make yourself easy about that there, my dear", replied the little man. "If he was so much as to move an inch without leave, Green would jist fetch him a crack over the head with the telescope, as would send him to the bottom of the basket in no time, and stun him till they come down again."

"Would he though?" inquired the other man.

"Yes, would he", replied the little one, "and think nothing of it, neither, if he was the king himself. Green's presence of mind is wonderful."

Just at this moment all eyes were directed to the preparations which were being made for starting. The car was attached to the second balloon, the two were brought pretty close together, and a military band commenced playing, with a zeal and fervour which would render the most timid man in existence but too happy to accept any means of quitting that particular spot of earth on which they were stationed. Then Mr. Green, sen., and his noble companion entered one car, and Mr. Green, jun., and *his* companion the other; and then the balloons went up, and the aerial travellers stood up, and the crowd outside roared with delight, and the two gentlemen who had never ascended before, tried to wave their flags, as if they were not nervous, but held on very fast all the while; and the balloons were wafted gently away, our little friend solemnly protesting, long after they were reduced to mere specks in the air, that he could still distinguish the white hat of Mr. Green. The gardens disgorged their multitudes, boys ran up and down screaming "bal-loon"; and in all the crowded thoroughfares people rushed out of their shops into the middle of the road, and having stared up in the air at two little black objects till they almost dislocated their necks, walked slowly in again, perfectly satisfied.

The next day there was a grand account of the ascent in the morning papers, and the public were informed how it was the finest day but four in Mr. Green's remembrance; how they retained sight of the earth till they lost it behind the clouds; and how the reflection of the balloon on the undulating masses of vapour was gorgeously picturesque; together with a little science about the refraction of the sun's rays, and some mysterious hints respecting atmospheric heat and eddying currents of air.

There was also an interesting account how a man in a boat was distinctly heard by Mr. Green, jun., to exclaim, "My eye!" which Mr. Green, jun., attributed to his voice rising to the balloon, and the sound being thrown back from its surface into the car; and the whole concluded with a slight allusion to another ascent next Wednesday, all of which was very instructive and very amusing, as our readers will see if they look to the papers. If we have forgotten to mention the date, they have only to wait until next summer, and take the account of the first ascent, and it will answer the purpose equally well.

Sketches by Boz

Mrs. E. S. Sheppard

EARLY VICTORIAN MINIATURE

TURNING OUT of the Market Place, a narrow street presented itself; here were factories and the backs of houses. Again we threaded a narrow turning; here was an outskirt of the town. It fronted a vast green space; all building-ground enclosed this quiet corner, for only a few small houses stood about. Here were no shops, no traffic. We went on in all haste, and soon my guide arrested himself at a small green gate. He unlatched it; we passed through into a tiny garden, trim as tiny, pretty as trim, and enchantingly after my own way of thinking. Never shall I forget its aspect; the round bed in the centre edged with box as green as moss; the big rose-tree in the middle of the bed, and lesser rosetrees round; the narrow gravel walk, quite golden in the sun; the outer edge of box, the outer bed of heaths and carnations, and glowing purple stocks. But above all the giant hollyhocks, one on each side of a little brown door, whose little latticed porch was arched with clematis, silvery as if moonlight "Minatrost" were ever brooding upon the threshold.

I must not loiter here; it would have been difficult to loiter in going about the garden, it was so unusually small; and the house, if possible was more diminutive. It had above the door two tiny casement windows. Only two; and as my guide opened the door with a key he brought out of his pocket, there was nothing to delay our entrance. The passage was very narrow, but lightsome, for a door was open at the end, peeping into a lawny kind of yard. No children were tumbling about, nor was there any kitchen smell, but the rarest of all essences, a just perceptible cleanliness—not moisture, but freshness.

We advanced to a staircase about three feet in width, uncarpeted, but of a rich brown colour, like chestnut skins; so also were the balusters. About a dozen steps brought us to a proportionate landing-place, and here I beheld two other little brown doors at angles with one another. Lenhart Davy opened one of these, and led me into a tiny room. Oh! what a tiny room! It was so tiny, so rare, so curiously perfect, that I could not help looking into it as I should have done into a cabinet collection. The casements were uncurtained, but a green silk shade, gathered at the top and bottom, was drawn half way along each. The walls were entirely books—in fact, the first thing I thought of was the book-houses I used to build of all the odd volumes in our parlour closet, during my quite incipient years. But such books as adorned the sides of the little sanctum were more suitable for walls than mine, in respect of size, being as they were, or as far as I could see, all music books, except in a stand between the casements, where a few others rested one against another. There was a soft grey drugget upon the floor; and though, of course, the book walls took up as much as half the room (a complete inner coat they made for the outside shell), yet it did not strike me as poking, because there was no heavy furniture—only a table, rather oval than round, and four chairs; both chairs and table of the hue I had admired on the staircase—a rich vegetable brown. On the table stood a square inkstand of the same wood, and a little tray filled with such odds as rubber, a penknife, sealing wax, and a pencil. The wood of the mantel-shelf was of the same tone, and so was that of a plain piano that stood to the left of the fireplace, in the only nook that was not books from floor to ceiling; but the books began again over the piano. All this wood, so darkly striking to the eye, had an indescribably soothing effect, (upon me I mean) and right glad was I to see Mr. Davy seat himself upon a little brown bench before the piano, and open it carefully.

"Will you take off your hat for a minute or two, my dear boy?" he asked, before he did anything else.

I laid the beaver upon the oval table.

"Now, tell me, can you sing at all?"

"Yes, Sir."

"From notes, or by ear?"

"A great deal by ear, but pretty well by notes."

"*From* notes", he said, correctingly, and I laughed.

He then handed me a little book of chorales, which he fetched from some out of the way hole beneath the instrument. They were all German. I knew some of them well enough.

"Oh, yes, I can sing these, I think."

"Try '*Ein' feste Burg ist unser Herr.*' Can you sing alto?"

"I always do. Millicent says it is proper for boys."

He just played the opening chord *slentando*, and I began. I was perfectly comfortable, because I knew what I was about, and my voice, as a child's, was perfect. I saw, by his face, that he was very surprised, as well as pleased. Then he left me alone to sing another, and then a third, but at last he broke in with a bass, the purest, mellowest, and most unshaken, I have ever heard, though not strong; neither did he derange me by a florid accompaniment he made as we went along. When I had concluded the fourth, he turned, and took my hand in his.

"I knew you could do something for music, but I had no idea it would be so very sweetly. I believe you will go to the Festival, after all. You perceive that I am very poor, or perhaps you do not perceive it, for children see fairies in flies. But look round my little room. I have nothing valuable except my books and piano, and those I bought with all the money I had several years ago. I dare say that you think my house is pretty. Well, it was just as bare as a barn when I came here six months ago. I made the shelves (the houses for my precious books) of deal, and I made that table, and the chairs, and this bench, of deal, and stained each afterwards; I stained my shelves, too, and my piano. I only tell you this that you may understand how poor I am. I cannot afford to give you one of those tickets, they are too dear; neither have I one myself; but if your mother approves, and you like it, I believe I can take you with me to sing in the chorus."

This was too much for me to bear without some strong expression or other. I took my hat, hid my face in it, and then threw my arms round Lenhart Davy's neck. He kissed me as a young father might have done, with a sort of pride, and I was able to perceive he had taken an instant fancy to me. I did not ask him whether he led the chorus, nor what he had to do with it, nor what I should have to do, but I begged him joyously to take me home directly. He tied on my hat himself, and I scampered all the way downstairs and round the garden before he came out of his shell. He soon followed me, smiling; and though he asked me no curious question as we went along, I could tell he was nervous about something. We walked very fast, and in a little less than an hour from the time I left home, I stood again upon the threshold.

Charles Auchester, Ch. 4

Benjamin Disraeli

THE TEMPLE OF THE MUSES

GERARD AND STEPHEN stopped before a tall, thin, stuccoed house, balustraded and friezed, very much lighted both within and without, and, from the sounds that issued from it, and the persons who retired and entered, evidently a locality of great resort and bustle. A sign, bearing the title of the Cat and Fiddle, indicated that it was a place of public entertainment, and kept by one who owned the legal name of John Trottman, though that was but a vulgar appellation, lost in his well-earned and far-famed title of Chaffing Jack.

The companions entered the spacious premises; and making their way to the crowded bar, Stephen, with a glance serious but which indicated intimacy, caught the eye of a comely lady, who presided over the mysteries, and said in a low voice, "Is he here?"

"In the Temple, Mr. Morley, asking for you and your friend more than once. I think you had better go up. I know he wishes to see you."

Stephen whispered to Gerard, and after a moment's pause he asked the fair president for a couple of tickets, for each of which he paid threepence; a sum, however, according to the printed declaration on the voucher, convertible into potential liquid refreshments, no great compensation to a member of the Temperance Society of Mowbray.

A handsome staircase with bright brass banisters led them to an ample landing-place, on which opened a door, now closed, and by which sat a boy who collected the tickets of those who would enter it. The portal was of considerable dimensions and of architectural pretension; it was painted of a bright green colour, the panels gilt. Within the pediment, described in letters of flaming gas, you read, "THE TEMPLE OF THE MUSES".

Gerard and Morley entered an apartment very long and sufficiently lofty, though rather narrow for such proportions. The ceiling was even richly decorated; the walls were painted, and by a brush of considerable power. Each panel represented some well-known scene from Shakespeare, Byron, or Scott: King Richard, Mazeppa, the Lady of the Lake were easily recognised: in one panel, Hubert menaced Arthur; here Haidee rescued Juan; and there Jeanie Deans curtsied before the Queen. The room was very full; some three or four hundred persons were seated in different groups at different tables, eating, drinking, talking, laughing, and even smoking, for notwithstanding the pictures and the gilding it was found impossible to forbid, though there were efforts to discourage, this practice, in the Temple of the Muses. Nothing, however, could be more decorous than the general conduct of the company, though they consisted principally of factory people. The waiters flew about with as much agility as though they were serving nobles. In general the noise was great, though not disagreeable; sometimes a bell rang and there was comparative silence, while a curtain drew up at the further end of the room, opposite the entrance, and where there was a theatre, the stage raised at a due elevation, and adorned with side scenes from which issued a lady in a fancy dress who sang a favourite ballad; or a gentleman elaborately habited in a farmer's costume of the old comedy, a bob-wig, silver buttons and buckles, and blue stockings, and who favoured the company with that melancholy effusion called a comic song. Some nights there was music on the stage; a young lady in a white robe with a golden harp, and attended by a gentleman in black mustachios. This was when the principal harpist of the King of Saxony and his first fiddler happened to be passing through Mowbray, merely by accident, or on a tour of pleasure and instruction, to witness the famous scenes of British industry. Otherwise the audience of the Cat and Fiddle, we mean the Temple of the Muses, were fain to be content with four Bohemian brothers, or an equal number of Swiss sisters. The most popular amusements however were the "Thespian recitations"; by amateurs, or novices who wished to become professional. They tried their metal on an audience which could be critical.

A sharp waiter, with a keen eye on the entering guests, immediately saluted Gerard and his friend, with profuse offers of hospitality: insisting that they wanted much refreshment; that they were both very hungry and very thirsty; that, if not hungry, they should order something to drink, that would give them an appetite; if not inclined to quaff, something to eat that would make them athirst. In the midst of these embarrassing attentions, he was pushed aside by his master with, "There, go; hands wanted at the upper end; two American gentlemen from Lowell singing out for Sherry-cobbler; don't know what it is; give them our bar mixture; if they complain say it's Mowbray slap-bang, and no mistake. Must have a name, Mr. Morley; name's everything; made the fortune of the Temple; if I had called it the Saloon, it never would have filled, and perhaps the magistrates never have granted a licence."

The speaker was a very portly man who had passed the

maturity of manhood, but active as Harlequin. He had a well-favoured countenance; fair, good-humoured, but very sly. He was dressed like the head butler of a London Tavern, and was particular as to his white waistcoats and black silk stockings, punctilious as to his knee-buckles, proud of his diamond pin; that is to say when he officiated at the Temple. . . .

"Hush!" said their host as a bell sounded, and he jumped up. "Now ladies, now gentlemen, if you please; silence if you please for a song from a Polish lady. The Signora sings English like a new-born babe"; and the curtain drew up amid the hushed voices of the company and the restrained clatter of their knives and forks and glasses.

The Polish lady sang "Cherry Ripe" to the infinite satisfaction of her audience. Young Mowbray indeed, in the shape of Dandy Mick and some of his followers and admirers, insisted on an encore. The lady as she retired curtsied like a Prima Donna; but the host continued on his legs for some time, throwing open his coat and bowing to his guests, who expressed by their applause how much they approved his enterprise. At length he resumed his seat; "It's almost too much", he exclaimed; "the enthusiasm of these people. I believe they look on me as a father."

In the meantime, we must not forget Dandy Mick and his two young friends whom he had so generously offered to treat to the Temple.

"Well, what do you think of it?" asked Caroline of Harriet; in a whisper as they entered the splendid apartment.

"It's just what I thought the Queen lived in", said Harriet; "but indeed I'm all of a flutter."

"Well, don't look as if you were", said her friend.

"Come along, gals", said Mick; "who's afraid? Here, we'll sit down at this table. Now, what shall we have? Here, waiter; I say, waiter!"

"Yes, sir; yes, sir."

"Well, why don't you come when I call?" said Mick with a

consequential air. "I have been hallooing these ten minutes.
Couple of glasses of bar mixture for these ladies and a go of gin
for myself. And I say, waiter, stop, stop, don't be in such a
deuced hurry; do you think folks can drink without eating?—
sausages for three; and damme, take care they are not burnt."

"Yes, sir, directly, directly."

"That's the way to talk to these fellows", said Mick with a
self-satisfied air, and perfectly repaid by the admiring gaze of
his companions.

"It's pretty, Miss Harriet", said Mick, looking up at the ceiling
with a careless *nil admirari* glance.

"Oh! it is beautiful", said Harriet.

"You never were here before; it's the only place. That's the
Lady of the Lake", he added, pointing to a picture; "I've seen
her at the circus, with real water".

The hissing sausages crowning a pile of mashed potatoes were
placed before them; the delicate rummers of the Mowbray
slap-bang, for the girls; the more masculine pewter measure
for their friend.

"Are the plates very hot?" said Mick.

"Very, sir."

"Hot plates half the battle", said Mick.

"Now, Caroline; here, Miss Harriet; don't take away your
plate, wait for the mash; they mash their taters here very elegant."

It was a very happy and very merry party. Mick delighted to
help his guests, and to drink their healths.

"Well," said he, when the waiter had cleared away their plates,
and left them to their less substantial luxuries. "Well", said
Mick, supping a renewed glass of gin twist and leaning back in
his chair, "say what you please, there's nothing like life."

"At the Traffords' ", said Caroline, "the greatest fun we ever
had was a singing class."

"I pity them poor devils in the country", said Mick; "we got
some of them at Collinson's—come from Suffolk they say;
what they call hagricultural labourers, a very queer lot indeed."

"Ah! them's the himmigrants", said Caroline; "they're sold

out of slavery, and sent down by Pickford's van into the labour market to bring down wages."

"We'll teach them a trick or two before they do that", said Mick. "Where are you, Miss Harriet?"

"I'm at Wiggins and Webster's, sir."

"Where they clean machinery during meal-time; that won't do", said Mick. "I see one of your partners coming in", said Mick, making many signals to a person who very soon joined them. "Well, Devilsdust, how are you?! . . .

Devilsdust had entered life so early that at seventeen he combined the experience of manhood with the divine energy of youth. He was a first-rate workman and received high wages; he had availed himself of the advantages of the factory school; he soon learnt to read and write with facility, and at the moment of our history was the leading spirit of the Shoddy-Court Literary and Scientific Institute. His great friend, his only intimate, was Dandy Mick. The apparent contrariety of their qualities and structure perhaps led to this. It is indeed the most assured basis of friendship. Devilsdust was dark and melancholy; ambitious and discontented; full of thought, and with powers of patience and perseverance that alone amounted to genius. Mick was as brilliant as his complexion; gay, irritable, evanescent, and unstable. Mick enjoyed life; his friend only endured it; yet Mick was always complaining of the lowness of his wages and the greatness of his toil; while Devilsdust never murmured, but read and pondered on the rights of labour, and sighed to vindicate his order.

"I have some thoughts of joining the Total Abstinence", said Devilsdust; "ever since I read Stephen Morley's address it has been in my mind. We shall never get our rights until we leave off consuming excisable articles; and the best thing to begin with is liquors."

"Well, I could do without liquors myself", said Caroline. "If I was a lady, I would never drink anything except fresh milk from the cow."

"Tea for my money", said Harriet; "I must say there's nothing

I grudge for good tea. Now I keep house, I mean always to drink the best."

"Well, you have not yet taken the pledge, Dusty", said Mick; "and so suppose we order a go of gin and talk this matter of temperance over. . . . "

"The people won't bear their grievances much longer", said Devilsdust.

"I think one of the greatest grievances the people have", said Caroline, "is the beaks serving notice on Chaffing Jack to shut up the Temple on Sunday nights."

"It is infamous", said Mick; "ain't we to have no recreation? One might as well live in Suffolk, where the immigrants come from, and where they are obliged to burn ricks to pass the time."

"As for the rights of labour", said Harriet, "the people goes for nothing with this machinery."

"And you have opened your mouth to say a very sensible thing, Miss Harriet", said Mick; "but if I were Lord Paramount for eight-and-forty hours, I'd soon settle that question. Wouldn't I fire a broadside into their 'double deckers'? The battle of Navarino at Mowbray fair with fourteen squibs from the Admiral's ship going off at the same time, should be nothing to it."

"Labour may be weak, but Capital is weaker", said Devilsdust. "Their capital is all paper."

"I tell you what", said Mick, with a knowing look, and in a lowered tone, "the only thing, my hearties, that can save this here nation, is—a - - - good strike."

Sybil, or the Two Nations, Ch. 10

Charles Kingsley

THE HOLINESS OF MUSIC

"And suddenly there was with the angel a multitude of the heavenly host, praising God, and saying: 'Glory to God in the highest, and on earth peace, goodwill towards men'."

YOU HAVE been just singing Christmas hymns, and my text speaks of the first Christmas hymn. Now, what the words of that hymn meant, what peace on earth and goodwill towards men meant, I have often told you. Today I want you for once to think of this—that it was a hymn that these angels were singing, even as human beings sing.

There is something very wonderful in music. Words are wonderful enough, but music is even more wonderful. It speaks not to our thoughts as words do;—it speaks to our hearts and spirits—to the very core and root of our souls. Music soothes us, stirs us up; it puts noble feelings in us; it melts us to tears— we know not how. It is a language by itself, just as perfect in its way as speech; as words; just as divine; just as blessed. . . .

Music, I say, *without* words, is wonderful and blessed; one of God's best gifts to man. But in singing you have both the wonders together—music and words. Singing speaks at once to the head and the heart—to our understanding and our feelings; and therefore, perhaps, the most beautiful way in which the reasonable soul of man can show itself (except, of course, by doing right, which always is, and always will be, the most beautiful thing) is singing.

Now, why do we all enjoy music? Because it sounds sweet. But why does it sound sweet?

That is a mystery known only to God.

Two things I will make you understand: two things which help to make music—melody and harmony.

Now, as most of you know, there is melody in music when the different sounds of the same tune follow each other so as to give us pleasure; there is harmony in music when different sounds, instead of following each other, come at the same time so as to give us pleasure.

But why do they please us? And what is more, why do they please angels? And still more—why do they please God? Why is there music in heaven? Consider St. John's visions in the Revelations. Why did St. John hear therein harpers with their harps, and the mystic beasts, and the elders, singing a new song to God and to the Lamb, and the voices of many angels round about them, whose number was ten thousand times ten thousand?

There is music in heaven because in music there is no self-will. Music goes on certain laws and rules. Man did not make these rules of music, he has only found them out. And if he be self-willed and break them, there is an end to his music instantly: all he brings out is discord and ugly sounds. The greatest musician in the world is as much bound by those laws as the learner in the school; and the greatest is the one who, instead of fancying that because he is clever he may throw aside the laws of music, knows the laws of music best, and observes them most reverently. And therefore it was that the old Greeks, the wisest of all the heathens, made a point of teaching their children music; because, they said, it taught them not to be self-willed and fanciful, but to see the beauty of order, the usefulness of rule, the divineness of laws.

And therefore music is fit for heaven; therefore music is a pattern and type of heaven, and the everlasting life of God, which perfect spirits live in heaven; a life of melody and order in themselves; a life of harmony with each other and God. Music, I say, is a pattern of the everlasting life of heaven, because in heaven as in music, is perfect freedom and perfect pleasure. And yet that freedom comes not from throwing away law, but from obeying God's law perfectly; and that pleasure comes not from self-will, and each doing what he likes, but perfectly doing the will of the Father who is in heaven.

And that in itself would be sweet music, even if there were neither voice nor sound in heaven. For wherever there is order and obedience, there is sweet music for the ears of Christ. Whatsoever does its duty, according to its kind which Christ has given it, makes melody in the ears of Christ. Whatsoever is useful to the things around it, makes harmony in the ears of Christ. . . .

Go home, then, remembering how divine and holy a thing music is, and rejoice before the Lord this day with psalms, and hymns, and spiritual songs (by which last I think the apostle means not merely church music, but songs which have a good and wholesome spirit in them) and remembering, too, that music, like marriage and all other beautiful things which God has given to man, is not to be taken in hand unadvisedly, lightly, or wantonly, but even when it is most cheerful and joyful (as marriage is) reverently, discreetly, soberly, and in the fear of God. Amen.

From a Christmas sermon

Thomas Carlyle

THE GIFTED

"MAN OF GENIUS?" Thou hast small notion, meseems, O Mecaenas Twiddledee, of what a Man of Genius is. Read in thy New Testament and elsewhere,—if, with floods of mealymouthed inanity, with miserable froth-vortices of Cant now several centuries old, thy New Testament is not all bedimmed for thee. *Canst* thou read in thy New Testament at all? The Highest Man of Genius, knowest thou him; Godlike and a God to this hour? His crown a Crown of Thorns? Thou fool, with *thy* empty Godhoods, Apotheoses *edgegilt;* the Crown of Thorns made into a poor jewel-room crown, fit for the head of blockheads; the bearing of the Cross changed to a riding in the Long-Acre Gig! Pause in thy mass-chantings, in thy litanyings, and Calmuck prayings by machinery; and pray, if noisily, at least in a more human manner. How with thy rubrics and dalmatics, and cloth-webs and cobwebs, and with thy stupidities and grovelling baseheartedness, hast thou hidden the Holiest into all but invisibility!—

"Man of Genius:" O Mecaenas Twiddledee, hast thou any notion what a Man of Genius is? Genius is "the inspired gift of God". It is the clearer presence of God Most High in a man. Dim, potential in all men; in this man it has become clear, actual. So says John Milton, who ought to be a judge; so answer him the Voices of all Ages and all Worlds. Would'st thou commune with such a one? *Be* his real peer then: does that lie in thee?

The attachments, the antipathies and the hospitalities of the district are ardent, hearty, and homely. Cordiality in each is the prominent characteristic. As a people, these mountaineers have ever been accessible to gentleness and truth, so far as I have known them; but excite suspicion or resentment, and they give emphatic and not impotent resistance. Compulsion they defy."

The Life of Charlotte Brontë

Charles Reade

A DRAMATIC MUSICIAN

THERE DIED the other day in London a musician, who used to compose, or set, good music to orchestral instruments, and play it in the theatre with spirit and taste, and to watch the stage with one eye and the orchestra with another, and so accompany with vigilant delicacy a mixed scene of action and dialogue; to do which the music must be full when the actor works in silence, but subdued promptly as often as the actor speaks. Thus it enhances the action without drowning a spoken line.

These are varied gifts, none of them common, and music is a popular art. One would think, then, that such a composer and artist would make his fortune nowadays. Not so. Mr. Edwin Ellis lived sober, laborious, prudent, respected, and died poor. He was provident and insured his life; he had a family and so small an income that he could not keep up the insurance. He has left a wife and nine children utterly destitute, and he could not possibly help it. The kindest-hearted profession in the world —though burdened with many charitable claims—will do what it can for them; but I do think the whole weight ought not to fall upon actors and musicians. The man was a better servant of the public than people are aware, and therefore I ask leave to say a few words to the public and to the Press over his ill-remunerated art, and his untimely grave.

Surely the prizes of the theatre are dealt too unevenly, when such a man for his compositions and his performance receives not half the salary of many a third class performer on the stage, works his heart out, never wastes a shilling, and dies without one?

No individual is to blame; but the system seems indiscriminating and unjust, and arises from a special kind of ignorance, which is very general, but I think and hope is curable.

Dramatic effects are singularly complex, and they cannot really be understood unless they are decomposed. But it is rare to find, out of the theatre, a mind accustomed to decompose them. The writer is constantly blamed for the actor's misinterpretation, and the actor for the writer's feebleness. Indeed, the general inability to decompose and so discriminate goes so far as this—you hear an author gravely accused by a dozen commentators of writing a new play four hours long. Of those four hours the stage-carpenter occupied one hour and thirty minutes. Yet they ascribe that mechanic's delay to the lines and delivery, when all the time it was the carpenter, who had not rehearsed his part, and therefore kept the author and the actors waiting just as long as he did the audience.

Where the habit of decomposing effects is so entirely absent, it follows, as a matter of course, that the subtle subsidiary art of the able leader is not distinguished, and goes for nothing in the public estimate of a play. I suppose two million people have seen Shaun the Post escape from his prison by mounting the ivied tower, and have panted at the view. Of those two million how many are aware that they saw with the ear as well as the eye, and that much of their emotion was caused by a mighty melody, such as effeminate Italy never produced—and never will till she breeds more men and less monks—being played all the time on the great principle of climax, swelling higher and higher, as the hero of the scene mounted and surmounted? Not six in the two million spectators, I believe. Mr. Ellis has lifted scenes and situations for me and other writers scores of times, and his share of the effect never been publicly noticed. When he had a powerful action of impassioned dialogue to illustrate he did not habitually run to the poor resource of a "hurry" or a nonsense

as to give me the following remarks:—"The question, what is the essence of musical 'expression' involves a number of obscure points, which, so far as I am aware, are as yet unsolved enigmas. Up to a certain point, however, any law which is found to hold as to the expression of the emotions by simple sounds must apply to the more developed mode of expression in song, which may be taken as the primary type of all music. A great part of the emotional effect of a song depends on the character of the action by which the sounds are produced. In songs, for instance, which express great vehemence of passion, the effect often chiefly depends on the forcible utterance of some one or two characteristic passages which demand great exertion of vocal force; and it will be frequently noticed that a song of this character fails in its proper effect when sung by a voice of insufficient power and range to give the characteristic passages without much exertion. This is, no doubt, the secret of the loss of effects so often produced by the transposition of a song from one key to another. The effect is thus seen to depend not merely on the actual sound, but also in part on the nature of the action which produces the sounds. Indeed it is obvious that whenever we feel the 'expression' of a song to be due to its quickness or slowness of movement—to smoothness of flow, loudness of utterance, and so forth—we are, in fact, interpreting the muscular actions which produce sound, in the same way in which we interpret muscular action generally. But this leaves unexplained the more subtle and more specific effect which we call the *musical* expression of the song—the delight given by its melody, or even by the separate sounds which make up the melody. This is an effect indefinable in language— one which, so far as I am aware, no one has been able to analyse, and which the ingenious speculation of Mr. Herbert Spencer as to the origin of music leaves quite unexplained. For it is certain that the *melodic* effect of a series of sounds does not depend in the least on their loudness or softness, or on their *absolute* pitch. A tune is always the same tune, whether it is sung loudly or softly, by a child or a man; whether it is played on a flute or on a trombone. The purely musical effect of any sound depends on its place in what is technically called a 'scale'; the same sound producing absolutely different effects on the ear, according as it is heard in connection with one or another series of sounds.

"It is on this *relative* association of the sounds that all the essentially characteristic effects which are summed up in the phrase 'musical expression' depend. But why certain associations of sounds have such-and-such effects, is a problem which yet remains to be solved. These effects must indeed, in some way or other, be connected with the well-known arithmetical relations between the rates of vibration of the sounds that form a musical scale. And it is possible—but this is merely a suggestion —that the greater or less mechanical facility with which the vibrating apparatus of the human larynx passes from one state of vibration to another, may have been a primary cause of the greater or less pleasure produced by various sequences of sounds."

But leaving aside these complex questions and confining ourselves to the simpler sounds, we can, at least, see some reasons for the association of certain kinds of sounds with certain states of mind. A scream, for instance, uttered by a young animal, or by one of the members of a community, as a call for assistance, will naturally be loud, prolonged, and high, so as to penetrate to a distance. For Helmholtz has shown that, owing to the shape of the internal cavity of the human ear and its consequent power of resonance, high notes produce a particularly strong impression. When male animals utter sounds in order to please the females, they would naturally employ those which are sweet to the ears of the species; and it appears that the same sounds are often pleasing to widely different animals, owing to the similarity of their nervous systems, as we ourselves perceive in the singing of birds and even in the chirping of certain treefrogs giving us pleasure. On the other hand, sounds produced in order to strike terror to an enemy, would naturally be harsh or displeasing.

Whether the principle of antithesis has come into play with sounds, as might perhaps have been expected, is doubtful. The interrupted, laughing or tittering sounds made by man and by various kinds of monkeys when pleased, are as different as possible

harmonies that came crashing overhead and round. Then there was one who touched me on the shoulder, and said, "Do you not see? it is Handel";—but I had hardly apprehended, and was trying to scale the terraces, and get near him, when I awoke, dazzled with the vividness and distinctness of the dream.

A piece of wood had burned through, and the ends had fallen into the ashes with a blaze: this, I suppose, had both given me my dream and robbed me of it. I was bitterly disappointed, and sitting up on my elbow, came back to reality and my strange surroundings as best I could.

I was thoroughly aroused—moreover, I felt a foreshadowing as though my attention were arrested by something more than the dream, though no sense in particular was as yet appealed to. I held my breath and waited, and then I heard—was it fancy? Nay; I listened again and again, and I *did* hear a faint and extremely distant sound of music, like that of an Aeolian harp, borne upon the wind which was blowing fresh and chill from the opposite mountains.

The roots of my hair thrilled. I listened, but the wind had died; and, fancying that it must have been the wind itself—on a sudden I remembered the noise which Chowbok had made in the wool-shed. Yes; it was that.

After a slow but steady climb of between three and four hours, during which I met with no serious hindrance, I found myself upon a tableland, and close to a glacier which I recognised as marking the summit of the pass. Above it towered a succession of rugged precipices and snowy mountain sides.

The solitude was greater than I could bear; the mountain upon my master's sheep-run was a crowded thoroughfare in comparison with this sombre sullen place. The air, moreover, was dark and heavy, which made the loneliness even more oppressive. There was an inky gloom over all that was not covered with snow and ice. Grass there was none.

Each moment I felt increasing upon me that dreadful doubt as to my own identity—as to the continuity of my past and present existence—which is the first sign of that distraction which comes on those who have lost themselves in the bush. I had fought against this feeling hitherto, and had conquered it; but the intense silence and gloom of this rocky wilderness were too much for me, and I felt that my power of collecting myself was beginning to be impaired.

I rested for a little while, and then advanced over very rough ground, until I reached the lower end of the glacier. Then I saw another glacier, decending from the eastern side to a small lake. I passed along the western side of the lake, where the ground was easier, and when I had got about half way I expected I should see the plains which I had already seen from the opposite mountains; but it was not to be so, for the clouds rolled up to the summit of the pass, though they did not overlip it on to the side from which I had come. I therefore soon found myself enshrouded by a cloud of thin vapour, which prevented my seeing more than a few yards in front of me. Then I came upon a large patch of old snow, in which I could distinctly trace the half-melted tracks of goats—and in one place, as it seemed to me, there had been a dog following them. Had I lighted upon a land of shepherds? The ground, where not covered with snow, was so poor and stony, and there was so little herbage, that I could see no sign of a path or regular sheep-track. But I could not help feeling rather uneasy as I wondered what sort of a reception I might meet with if I were to come suddenly upon inhabitants. I was thinking of this, and proceeding cautiously through the mist, when I began to fancy that I saw some objects darker than the cloud looming in front of me. A few steps brought me nearer, and a shudder of unutterable horror ran through me when I saw a circle of gigantic forms, many times higher than myself, upstanding grim and grey through the veil of cloud before me.

I suppose I must have fainted, for I found myself sometime afterwards sitting upon the ground, sick and deadly cold. There were the figures, quite still and silent, seen vaguely through the thick gloom, but in human shape indisputably.

ears and noses, like people looking over a wall. The remainder, stalwart ruddy men and boys, were dressed mainly in snow-white smock-frocks, embroidered upon the shoulders and breasts in ornamental forms of hearts, diamonds, and zigzags. The cider-mug was emptied for the ninth time, the music-books were arranged, and the pieces finally decided upon. The boys in the meantime put the old horn-lanterns in order, cut candles into short lengths to fit the lanterns; and, a thin fleece of snow having fallen since the early part of the evening, those who had no leggings went to the stable and wound wisps of hay round their ankles to keep the insidious flakes from the interior of their boots.

Mellstock was a parish of considerable acreage, the hamlets composing it lying at a much greater distance from each other than is ordinarily the case. Hence several hours were consumed in playing and singing within hearing of every family, even if but a single air were bestowed on each. There was Lower Mellstock, the main village; half a mile from this were the church and vicarage, and a few other houses, the spot being rather lonely now, though in past centuries it had been the most thickly-populated quarter of the parish. A mile north-east lay the hamlet of Upper Mellstock, where the tranter lived; and at other points knots of cottages, besides solitary farmsteads and dairies.

Old William Dewy, with the violoncello, played the bass; his grandson Dick the treble violin; and Reuben and Michael Mail the tenor and second violins respectively. The singers consisted of four men and seven boys, upon whom devolved the task of carrying and attending to the lanterns, and holding the books open for the players. Directly music was the theme old William ever and instinctively came to the front.

"Now mind, neighbours", he said, as they all went out one by one at the door, he himself holding it ajar and regarding them with a critical face as they passed, like a shepherd counting out his sheep. "You two counter-boys, keep your ears open to Michael's fingering, and don't ye go straying into the treble part along o' Dick and his set, as ye did last year; and mind this especially when we be in "Arise, and hail". Billy Chimlen, don't you sing quite so raving mad as you fain would; and, all o' ye, whatever ye do, keep from making a great scuffle on the ground when we go in at people's gates; but go quietly, so as to strike up all of a sudden, like spirits."

"Farmer Ledlow's first?"

"Farmer Ledlow's first; the rest as usual."

"And, Voss", said the tranter terminatively, "you keep house here till about half-past two; then heat the metheglin and cider in the warmer you'll find turned up upon the copper; and bring it wi' the victuals to church-hatch, as th'st know."

Just before the clock struck twelve they lighted the lanterns and started. The moon, in her third quarter, had risen since the snowstorm; but the dense accumulation of snow-cloud weakened her power to a faint twilight which was rather pervasive of the landscape than traceable to the sky. The breeze had gone down, and the rustle of their feet and tones of their speech echoed with an alert rebound from every post, boundary-stone, and ancient wall they passed, even where the distance of the echo's origin was less than a few yards. Beyond their own slight noises nothing was to be heard save the occasional bark of foxes in the direction of Yalbury Wood, or the brush of a rabbit among the grass now and then as it scampered out of their way.

Most of the outlying homesteads and hamlets had been visited by about two o'clock; they then passed across the outskirts of a wooded park toward the main village, nobody being at home at the Manor. Pursuing no recognized track, great care was necessary in walking lest their face should come in contact with the low hanging boughs of the old lime-trees, which in many spots formed dense overgrowths of interlaced branches.

"Times have changed from the times they used to be", said Mail, regarding nobody can tell what interesting old panoramas with an inward eye, and letting his outward glance rest on the ground because it was as convenient a position as any. "People don't care much about us now! I've been thinking we must be almost the last left in the county of the old string players? Barrel-organs, and the things next door to 'em that you blow wi' your foot, have come in terribly of late years."

"Ay!" said Bowman shaking his head; and old William on seeing him did the same thing.

"More's the pity", replied another. "Time was—long and merry ago now!—when not one of the varmints was to be heard of; but it served some of the quires right. They should have stuck to strings as we did, and kept out clarinets, and done away with serpents. If you'd thrive in musical religion, stick to strings, says I."

"Strings be safe soul-lifters, as far as that do go", said Mr. Spinks.

"Yet there's worse things than serpents", said Mr. Penny. "Old things pass away, 'tis true; but a serpent was a good old note: a deep rich note was the serpent."

"Clar'nets, however, be bad at all times", said Michael Mail. "One Christmas—years agone now, years—I went the rounds wi' the Weatherbury quire. 'Twas a hard frosty night, and the keys of all the clar'nets froze—ah, they did freeze!—so that 'twas like drawing a cork every time a key was opened; and the players o' 'em had to go into a hedger-and-ditcher's chimley-corner, and thaw their clar'nets every now and then. An icicle o'spet hung down from the end of every man's clar'net a span long; and as to fingers—well, there, if ye'll believe me, we had no fingers at all, to our knowing."

"I can well bring back to my mind", said Mr. Penny, "what I said to poor Joseph Ryme (who took the treble part in Chalf-Newton Church for two-and-forty year) when they thought of having clar'nets there. 'Joseph', I said says I, 'depend upon't, if so be you have them tooting clar'nets you'll spoil the whole set-out. Clar'nets were not made for the service of the Lard; you can see it by looking at 'em', I said. And what came o't? Why, souls, the parson set up a barrel-organ on his own account within two years o'the time I spoke, and the old quire went to nothing."

"As far as look is concerned", said the tranter, "I don't for

my part see that a fiddle is much nearer heaven than a clar'net.
'Tis further off. There's always a rakish, scampish twist about a
fiddle's looks that seems to say the Wicked One had a hand in
making o'en; while angels be supposed to play clar'nets in heaven,
or som'at like 'em, if ye may believe picters".

"Robert Penny, you was in the right", broke in the eldest
Dewy. "They should ha' stuck to strings. Your brass-man is
a rafting dog—well and good; your reed-man is a dab at stirring
ye—well and good; your drum-man is a rare bowel-shaker—
good again. But I don't care who hears me say it, nothing will
spak to your heart wi' the sweetness o' the man of strings!"

"Strings for ever!" said little Jimmy.

"Strings alone would have held their ground against all the
new comers in creation." ("True, true!" said Bowman.) "But
clarinets was death." ("Death they was" said Mr. Penny.)
"And harmonions", William continued in a louder voice, and
getting excited by these signs of approval, "harmonions and
barrel-organs" ("Ah!" and groans from Spinks) "be miserable—
what shall I call 'em?—miserable——"

"Sinners", suggested Jimmy, who made large strides like the
men and did not lag behind with the other little boys.

"Miserable dumbledores!"

"Right, William, and so they be—miserable dumbledores!"
said the choir with unanimity.

By this time they were crossing to a gate in the direction of the
school which, standing on a slight eminence at the junction of
three ways, now rose in unvarying and dark flatness against the
sky. The instruments were retuned, and all the band entered the
school enclosure, enjoined by old William to keep upon the
grass.

"Number seventy-eight", he softly gave out as they formed
round in a semi-circle, the boys opening the lanterns to get a
clearer light, and directing their rays on the books.

Then passed forth into the quiet night an ancient and time-
worn hymn, embodying a quaint Christianity in words orally
transmitted from father to son through several generations down

to the present characters, who sang them out right earnestly:

"Remember Adam's fall,
O thou Man:
Remember Adam's fall
From Heaven to Hell.
Remember Adam's fall;
How he hath condemn'd all
In Hell perpetual
There for to dwell.

Remember God's goodnesse,
O thou Man:
Remember God's goodnesse,
His promise made.
Remember God's goodnesse;
He sent His Son sinlesse
Our ails for to redress;
Be not afraid!

In Bethlehem He was born,
O thou Man:
In Bethlehem He was born,
For mankind's sake.
In Bethlehem He was born,
Christmas-day i' the morn:
Our Saviour thought no scorn
Our faults to take.

Give thanks to God alway,
O thou Man;
Give thanks to God alway
With heart-most joy.
Give thanks to God alway
On this our joyful day:
Let all men sing and say,
Holy, Holy!"

228

Having concluded the last note they listened for a minute or two, but found that no sound issued from the schoolhouse.

"Four breaths, and then, 'O, what unbounded goodness!' number fifty-nine", said William.

This was duly gone through, and no notice whatever seemed to be taken of the performance.

"God guide us, surely 'tisn't a' empty house, as befell us in the year thirty-nine and forty-three!" said old Dewy.

"Perhaps she's jist come from some musical city, and sneers at our doings?" the tranter whispered.

"'Od rabbit her!" said Mr. Penny, with an annihilating look at a corner of the school chimney, "I don't quite stomach her, if this is it. Your plain music well done is as worthy as your other sort done bad, a' b'lieve, souls; so say I."

"Four breaths, and then the last", said the leader authoritatively. 'Rejoice, ye Tenants of the Earth', number sixty-four."

At the close, waiting yet another minute, he said in a clear loud voice, as he had said in the village at that hour and season for the previous forty years—

"A merry Christmas to ye!"

Under the Greenwood Tree

Charles Willeby

THE COMPOSER OF "CARMEN"

WHAT LITTLE has been written about poor Bizet is not the sort to satisfy. The men who have told of him cannot have written with their best pen. Even those who, one can see, have started well, albeit impelled rather than inspired by a profound admiration for the artist and the man, have fallen all too short of the mark, and ultimately drifted into the dullest of all dull things—the compilation of mere dates and doings. I know of no pamphlet devoted to him in this country. He was much misunderstood in life; he has been, I think, as much sinned against in death. The symbol of posthumous appreciation which asserts itself to the visitor to Père Lachaise, is exponential of compliment only when reckoned by avoirdupois. Neglected in life, they have in death weighed him down with an edifice that would have been obnoxious to every instinct in his sprightly soul—a memorial befitting perhaps to such an one as Johannes Brahms, but repugnant as a memento of the spirit that created "Carmen". It is an emblem of French formalism in its most determined aspect. And in truth—as Sainte-Beuve said of the Abbé Galiani—"they owed to him an honourable, choice, and purely delicate burial; *urna brevis*, a little urn which should not be larger than he." The previous inappreciation of his genius has given place to posthumous laudation, zealous indeed, but so indiscriminating as to be vulgar. Like many another man, he had to take "a thrashing from life"; and although he stood up to it unflinchingly, it was only in his death certificate that he acquired passport to fame. . . .

Perhaps of all his powers Bizet's greatest was that of recuperation. It would be wrong to say he did not know defeat; he knew it all too well, but he never let it get the better of him. He was never without his iron upon the fire, never without a project to fall back upon. And perhaps it is not too much to say that he had no life outside his art. This too may in truth be told of him; that in all the struggle and the scramble, in all his fight with fortune, it was the sweeter qualities of his nature that came uppermost. His strength of purpose stood on a sound basis—a basis of confidence in, though not arrogance of, his own power. Where he was most handicapped was in carrying on his artistic progress *coram populo*. Had it been as gradual as most men's —had it been but the acquiring of an ordinary experience—all might have been well; he would probably have been accorded his niche and would have occupied it. But he progressed by leaps and bounds, and even then his ideal kept steadily miles ahead of his achievement. It was for long a very will-o'-the-wisp for him. Now and again he caught it, and it is at such moments that we have him at his best; but he can be said only to have captured it completely—so far as we are in a position to tell—in "L'Arlésienne" and certain parts of "Carmen". His faculty of self-criticism was developed in such an extraordinary degree as to baulk him. He loved this Don Rodrigue and thought it was his masterwork, and that too at the time when "Carmen" must have been well forward. We know then that the loss is not a small one.

It had not been alone the fate of the Opera House that had stood in the way. That institution had in course taken up its quarters at the Salle Ventadour, and once installed there had proceeded with the *répertoire*. But Bizet's "Rodrigue", although well backed by Fauré, was pushed aside for others. The three names that it bore were all too impotent; and when a new work was announced, it was "L'Esclave" of Membrée that was seen to grace the bills, and not "Don Rodrigue".

Poor Bizet, disappointed and sore at heart, vanished to hide himself once more by his beloved Seine. This time it was to Bougival he went.

M. Massenet had recently produced his "Marie Madeleine" and, curiously enough, it had been successful. This seems to have spurred Bizet on to emulation. With his usual happy knack of hitting on a subject, he wrote off to Gallet, requesting him to do a book with Geneviève de Paris—the holy Geneviève of Legendary lore—for heroine. And Gallet, accommodating creature that he was, forthwith proceeded to construct his tableaux. Together they went off to Lamoureux and read the synopsis to him. He approved it heartily, and Bizet got to work. "Carmen" was then finished and was undergoing the usual stage of adjournment *sine die*. Three times it had been put into rehearsal, only to be withdrawn for apparently no reason, and poor Bizet was wearying of opera and its ways. This sacred work was relief to him. But hardly had he settled down to it when up came "Carmen" once again, this time in good earnest. He was forced to leave "Geneviève" and come to Paris for rehearsals. It was much against his inclination that he did so, for his health was failing fast. For long he had suffered from an abscess which had made his life a burden to him. Nor had his terrible industry been without its effect upon his physique. He did not know it, but he had sacrificed to his work the very things he had worked for. He felt exhausted, enfeebled, shattered. Probably the excitement of rehearsing "Carmen" kept him up the while; but it had its after-effect, and the strain proved all the more disastrous. A profound melancholy, too, had come over him; and do what he would he could not beat it off. A young singer (some aspirant for lyric fame) came one day to sing to him. "Ich gröle nicht" and "Aus der Heimath" were chosen. "Quel chef d'oeuvre", said he, "mais, quelle désolation, c'est à vous donner la nostalgie de la mort". Then he sat down to the piano and played the "Marche Funèbre" of Chopin. That was the frame of mind he was in.

In his gayer moments he would often long for Italy. He had never forgotten the happy days passed there with Guiraud. "I dreamed last night" (he is writing to Guiraud) "that we were all at Naples, installed in a most lovely villa, and living under a government purely artistic. The Senate was made up by Beethoven, Michelangelo, Shakespeare, Giorgione, *e tutti quanti*. The National Guard was no more. In place of it there was a huge orchestra of which Litolff was the conductor. All suffrage was denied to idiots, humbugs, schemers, and ignoramuses, that is to say, suffrage was cut down to the smallest proportions imaginable. Geneviève was a little too amiable for Goethe, but despite this trifling circumstance the awakening was terribly bitter."

"Carmen" was produced at last, on the 3rd of March in that year (1875). The Habanera—of which, by the way, he wrote for Mme. Galli-Marié no less than thirteen versions before he came across, in an old book, the one we know—the prelude to the second act, the toreador song, and the quintette were encored. The rest fell absolutely flat.

The blow was a terrific one to Bizet. He had dreamed of such a different lot for "Carmen". Arm in arm with Guiraud he left the theatre, and together they paced the streets of Paris until dawn. Small wonder he felt bitter; and in vain the kindly Guiraud did his best to comfort him. Had not "Don Juan", he argued, been accorded a reception no whit better when it was produced in Vienna; and had not poor Mozart said "I have written 'Don Juan' for myself and two of my friends". But he found no consolation in the fact. The press, too, cut him to the quick. This "Carmen", said they, was immoral, *banale*; it was all head and no heart; the composer had made up his mind to show how learned he was, with the result that he was only dull and obscure. Then again, the gipsy girl whose liaisons formed the subject of the story was at best an odious creature; the actress's gestures were the very incarnation of vice, there was something licentious even in the tones of her voice; the composer evidently belonged to the school of *civet sans lièvre*; there was no unity of style; it was not dramatic, and could never live; in a word, there was no health in it.

Even Du Locke—who of all men should have supported it—played him false. A minister of the Government wrote personally to the director for a box for his family. Du Locke replied with an invitation to the rehearsal, adding that he had rather that the minister came himself before he brought his daughters.

Prostrate with it all, poor Bizet returned to Bougival. When forced to give up "Geneviève", he had written to Gallet: "I shall give the whole of May, June, and July to it." And now May was already come, and he was in his bed. "Angine colossale", were the words he sent to Guiraud, who was to have been with him the following Sunday. "Do not come as we arranged; imagine, if you can, a double pedal, A flat, E flat, straight through your head from left to right. This is how I am just now."

He never wrote more than a few pages of "Geneviève". He got worse and worse. But even so, the end came all too suddenly, and on the night of the 2nd of June he died—died as nearly as possible at the exact moment when Galli-Marié at the Opera Comique was singing her song of fate in the card scene of the third act of his "Carmen". The coincidence was true enough. That night it was with difficulty that she sung her song. Her nervousness, from some cause or another, was so great that it was with the utmost effort she pronounced the words: "La carte impitoyable; repetera la mort; encor, toujours la mort." On finishing the scene, she fainted at the wings. Next morning came the news of Bizet's death. And some friends said—because it was not meet for them to see the body—that the poor fellow had killed himself. Small wonder if it were so!

The Yellow Book, Vol. II, 1894

ALPHABETICAL LIST OF AUTHORS AND
WORKS QUOTED

AUTHOR	EXTRACT FROM
Addison, Joseph, 1672-1719	*The Spectator*
Austen, Jane, 1775-1817	*Pride and Prejudice*
Bacon, Sir Francis, 1561-1626	*Essays*
The Bible, Authorised Version, 1611	I Sam., Ch. XVI: v. 14-23, I Sam., Ch. XVIII: v. 5-12
Bisse, Dr. Thomas, d. 1731	Sermon preached at the Festival of the Three Choirs, Sept. 7th, 1726
Boswell, James, 1740-95	*Life of Dr. Johnson*
Bunyan, John, 1628-88	*The Pilgrim's Progress*
Burney, Dr. Charles, 1726-1814	*A General History of Music*
Burney, Fanny (Madame D'Arblay) 1752-1840	*Diary and Letters*
Burton, Sir Robert, 1577-1640	*Anatomy of Melaucholy*
Butler, Samuel, 1834-1902	*Erewhon*
Byrd, William, 1543-1623	Preface to *Psalmes, Sonets & Songs of Sadnes and Pietie*
Campian, Thomas, 1567-1619	*Description of a Maske*
Carlyle, Thomas, 1795-1881	*Past and Present*
Chesterfield, Fourth Earl of, 1694-1773	*Letter to his Son*
Cooper, Thomas, 1805-1892	*The Life of Thomas Cooper*
Darwin, Charles, 1809-1882	*The Expression of the Emotions in Man and Animals*
Defoe, Daniel, 1661-1731	*Tour of England and Wales*
Dibdin, Charles, 1745-1814	*The Life of Mr. Dibdin*
Dickens, Charles, 1812-70	*Sketches by Boz*
Disraeli, Benjamin, Earl of Beaconsfield, 1804-81	*Sybil, or The Two Nations*
Dryden, John, 1631-1700	Preface to *Albion and Albanius*
Fuller, Thomas, 1608-61	*History of the Worthies of England*
Gardiner, William, 1770-1853	*The Music of Nature*
Gaskell, Mrs. Elizabeth Cleghorn, 1810-65	*Life of Charlotte Brontë*
Goldsmith, Oliver, 1728-74	*The Vicar of Wakefield*
Hardy, Thomas, 1840-1928	*Under the Greenwood Tree*

Hawkins, Sir John, 1719-1789   Boyce's *Cathedral Music*
Hazlitt, William, 1778-1830   *The Examiner*, 1816
Hearne, Dr. Thomas, 1678-1735   *Remarks and Collections*
Jonson, Ben, 1573-1637   *Bartholomew Fair*
Kingsley, Charles, 1819-75   *Sermon*
Lamb, Charles, 1775-1834   *Essays of Elia*
Milton, John, 1608-74   *Tractate on Education*
Morley, Thomas, 1557-1603   *A Plaine and Easie Introduction to Practicall Musicke*

North, Roger, 1653-1734   *Memoires of Musicke*
Peacham, Henry, 1576?-1643?   *The Compleat Gentleman*
Pepys, Samuel, 1633-1703   *Diary*
Reade, Charles, 1814-84   *Readiana*
Scott, Sir Walter, 1771-1832   *Old Mortality*
Shakespeare, William, 1564-1616   *As You Like It*
Sheppard, Mrs. E. S. 1830-62   *Charles Auchester*
Sheridan, Richard Brinsley, 1751-1816   *A Trip to Scarborough*
Smollett, Tobias, 1721-71   *The Expedition of Humphry Clinker*

Walton, Izaak, 1593-1683   *Life of Mr. George Herbert*
Willeby, Charles   *The Yellow Book*
Wood, Anthony, 1632-95   *Life and Times of A. W.*